Groups:
Leadership and Group Development

Groups:
Leadership and Group Development

Hedley G. Dimock

University Associates, Inc.
8517 Production Avenue
San Diego, California 92121

Library of Congress Cataloging-in-Publication Data
Dimock, Hedley G. (Hedley Gardner)
    Groups: leadership and group development.

    Bibliography: p.
    1. Social groups.   2. Social group work.
I. Title.
HM131.D55   1986   302.3   86-30799
ISBN 0-88390-202-8

Cover Art: Linda Ouellette
Design & Layout: Carol Nolde and Ann Beaulieu

Preface

This book is for people working with groups in the human services—education, health services, recreation, and social welfare. These people share a common interest of trying to increase their effectiveness in helping groups to accomplish their tasks and in providing more growth and satisfaction for group members. During the twenty years since I first wrote this material, our society has become increasingly individually oriented. "Quality of life" in the work place, human rights, affirmative action programs, the women's movement, and minority group rights have been strong influences. And coupled with humanistic trends in education and institution treatment, permissiveness in child rearing, and a swing to a philosophy of self-fulfillment, the impact has been pervasive.

The rights and needs of individuals may conflict with the rights and needs of groups, yet as we'll see on the following pages, they can pull together toward common interests and goals. An understanding of the factors in working with groups suggests sound practices—no magic cure-alls—but effective approaches that have evolved from group research and the systematic evolution of field practices.

Many of the groups we'll consider have work to do and tasks to accomplish while others are vehicles for learning, growing, and development of the members. In both cases we'll look at helping you get the information you need about what's happening in the group, understand some of the major dynamics in play at that time, and assess the weaknesses and strengths of alternative actions. Hopefully, this will help you develop the results you want in your situations.

Hedley G. Dimock
October, 1986

Contents

Part 1:
Understanding
Group Behavior

Chapter 1

Understanding Group Leadership

The most important and exciting interest in a group is its leadership—who is providing it and how well it is working out. The way in which the leader works with the group, the impact of that style on the group's productivity, and the satisfaction and relationships of members have been the focus of continuous study for many years. Style of leadership has been found to be closely related to learning in classrooms, production in industry, achievement in team sports, growth in encounter groups, and task accomplishment in the military. Clearly an understanding of group leadership is a priority for everyone working with groups. Everyone has ideas about leadership— how people get to be leaders and what leaders should do to be successful and effective. Let's look at the understandings about leadership that will help us to put these divergent assumptions and attitudes into some perspective.

The earliest major theory of leadership was that in every group there was one leader and that this person was the leader because of certain leadership traits or leadership qualities. This was called the "great man" theory of leadership as it was believed that there were certain men (women were generally not included in this theory at that time) who possessed outstanding traits and abilities and who were destined to become great leaders. Alexander the Great, Hannibal, Julius Caesar, Benjamin Franklin, Napoleon, and Winston Churchill were frequently mentioned in this regard. The major events in history were also thought to have revolved around these great leaders and history could be best understood by studying these great people. It was thought, too, that these people were born with these outstanding qualities or traits and that they would be leaders regardless of the time or place in which they lived.

The question then was "what are these special traits that leaders have?" Early studies of leadership tried to identify these traits but every time a set of characteristics was identified and looked promising, it was found not to work out in other settings. The search for leadership traits has not worked out as years of research have been unable to find any consistent trait or personal characteristics which distinguish leaders from nonleaders. The conclusion has been that leaders do not have special personalities or traits, identifiable at this time, that separate them from other people. The "trait approach" or "leaders are born" theory has been generally abandoned because of a lack of scientific support. Yet many individuals continue to believe in it and continue, usually within the confines of their own work place, to seek out the characteristics that will identify their successful workers.

Leadership is now seen as a function of the situation—the type and difficulty of the task, the personality and competence of the members, and the power of the leader. This *situational leadership* theory assumes that leaders may have certain traits or skills that will increase the probability of their becoming a leader but these characteristics may be important only in that situation. As leadership is related to the situation there is a fair probability that the leader in one situation will be a leader in another very similar situation but not if the situation is different.

Our experiences usually confirm this idea that the person who is the leader in one situation may not be the leader in another. A university class may see Jane as the leader in a classroom discussion as she is articulate and knows her subject matter, while Susan takes over in the planning of the class's end-of-year party using her social skills and entertainment interests. In the work team the members may look to Estelle to help resolve a conflicted planning issue and to Charles to make up the complicated shift schedule for the next month. And as we look at United States history, we see some men who were outstanding military generals but who were not very effective presidents.

During World War II there was an increased interest in identifying potential leaders so they could be given special training to increase their effectiveness. The German army continued to develop its "leaderless discussion" technique to select men for officer's training. Candidates were assembled in small groups and given a general topic to discuss. No one was appointed leader but observers rated each participant's behavior on a series of scales. A high rating on leadership in this leaderless group was found to have a positive correlation with army performance. Later the British and American armies adopted this technique. The American army continued to use personality and performance tests but also experimented with numerous functional tests in selecting trainees for special missions overseas (OSS). These included stress situations such as frustrating instruction tasks, role playing and simulations of actual situations, and secret observation during parties and other informal situations.

These studies stimulated an interest in exploring the functions of leaders as leadership was seen as doing something to help a group solve a problem or accomplish an objective. Members perform leadership functions as they influence the behavior of other members and help the group achieve its goals. Most members of a group are "leaders" then at one time or another and we must study the group as a whole and identify patterns of leadership or frequency of leadership acts. Assumptions that one person was the leader and the rest were followers were discontinued in this functional, shared leadership approach.

FUNCTIONS OF GROUP LEADERS

The search for leadership functions continued in the late Forties and Fifties at Ohio State University with Navy funding. These studies shaped our understanding of leadership and are still the basis for the most widely accepted leadership theories. In these studies four factors appeared consistently to describe leadership behavior: showing consideration, initiating structure, a production emphasis, and social sensitivity. Showing consideration for other group members accounted for fifty percent of the leadership functions and initiating structure, thirty percent.

   The studies concluded that there are two basic leadership functions: (1) helping the group to acheive a specific goal; and (2) helping to maintain or build the group itself. Goal achievement or task accomplishment functions include: defining roles and expectations for members; establishing defined structures for operating; initiating action; providing expert information; and evaluating goal achievement progress.[1] Group building and maintenance functions were showing concern for individuals, facilitating open communication, providing support and encouragement, and stimulating self-direction.

   Again it is clear that many members in a group may perform these functions and some may even specialize in task functions while others contribute group-building behaviors. Many behaviors can contribute to goal achievement and group building at the same time. Providing top-notch plans for implementing a group task will not only increase goal achievement but also increase group solidarity and member satisfaction. Mediating a group conflict helps to maintain the group but also may free a log jam and move the group to accomplishing its task.

---

[1]An observation guide showing these functions is shown in Part 2, How to Observe Your Group.

Since the Ohio State studies a number of other investigations of leadership functions have rounded out the list but pretty much in the same areas. Stogdill (1974) summarized over fifty studies during a thirty-year period and came up with the following functions or characteristics.

Functions of an Effective Leader

Goal achievement

Technical skills
Administrative skills
Task motivation and application
Leadership achievement
Maintaining standards
  of performance

Group maintenance

Social and interpersonal skills
Social nearness, friendliness
Group task supportiveness
Maintaining cohesive work group
Facilitating coordination
  and teamwork

Intellectual and communication skills

OTHER CHARACTERISTICS OF LEADERS

In youth groups physical size has some relation to leadership potential and it is likely that this is related to athletic success where size may be an important factor. In adult situations size does not appear to be related to leadership, yet until the 1970s, police units in Canada had a minimum height and weight requirement, thinking that larger people got more respect (they gave it up when it was shown to discriminate against several minority groups, including native Canadians—and women). As the studies of functions have shown, leaders tend to have more intelligence, insight, initiative, soundness of judgment, and originality. They likely have more energy (better physical health), a better sense of humor, and a bit more tidy and attractive appearance than other members of the group.

It also appears that the person who does the most talking is most likely to influence the group and become accepted as leader as long as that person doesn't talk so much as to antagonize other members. Those who emerge as leaders are usually more vocal and dominant and this may help the group to move toward its goals. Certainly any member of a group who is the usual channel of communication, who has special access to people in power or influence related to the group's goals, or controls communication in any way is more likely to be a leader than one who does not. This explains why discussion leaders, group recorders or reporters, or those whose job or interests puts them into frequent contact with other members have a tendency to become leaders.

Fiedler (1967, 1974), in an extensive study of high school basketball teams and several adult groups, found that the leaders of the effective groups had greater social distance from their followers than the leaders of ineffective groups. Other studies also suggest that it may be better to be slightly aloof rather than "one of the gang." While Fiedler's later studies showed that the aloof leaders had a high goal achievement orientation and this helped them to have an effective group, it still seems social distance has some merits. While members still respect a leader with whom they are friendly and familiar, a leader who is too close to the members may find it difficult to realistically assess the strengths and weaknesses of individuals and may tend to make decisions based on general personal feelings.

For example, the captains of the winning basketball teams were able to differentiate among their teammates on a variety of personal and skill dimensions. They could describe a comprehensive set of weaknesses and strengths for each player and did not tend to describe several players in a similar way. They knew who could dribble the best, who played well under pressure, who was a team player and got others passing the ball around, and who to put into the game if the team was behind and needed a "spark plug" to get it clicking.

In the human relations training programs of our Centre we worked at helping human service workers develop these skills of being able to differentiate among their students or clients. During their training programs we asked them to write a brief thumbnail sketch of the other members of their training group, or to write three adjectives descriptive of each of the other members. To check the usefulness of these descriptions we asked participants to read their descriptions and see if the other members could detect who they were talking about. Many participants used the same descriptions in reference to several members. Clearly, they found it difficult to see other participants as unique individuals and likely in their concern for their own well being saw other members as "them." The participants who were able to describe others with such accuracy that other members could consistently recognize them usually were influential members or leaders in their groups. The need to be known and recognized as a unique person is an overwhelming motivation of adolescents, yet is a major concern of youth and adults. Anyone who can recognize and identify the unique attributes of others gains considerable respect and often leadership status in their groups. On-the-job studies have indicated that this is true of leaders, youth workers, counselors, and team leaders or managers.

LEADERSHIP AND THE GROUP

If leadership is best thought of as a group quality or set of functions which are needed for the group to operate effectively, then the interrelations among members must be studied to understand why certain members more frequently perform these functions. Or, to put it differently, leadership and the relation of the leader to followers cannot be looked at independently. The leader derives that position from the followers who see the leader as being able to help them to achieve this goal and maintain themselves as a group. The more a person helps other members accomplish their objectives, the more readily will these members accept that person's suggestions and they will likely look to that leader for further suggestions and help in building the solidarity of the group. Leaders may emerge as they appear to be able to provide for group needs or they may be selected because they control the means or resources (skills, knowledge, money, equipment, contacts, etc.) which the group needs to gain their objectives. Even if the leader is appointed by someone outside the group, the leader's status and acceptability will depend on the group's perspective of that person's ability to meet group needs or at least prevent reduced need satisfaction.

Accumulated studies have now made it clear that leadership is a function of group needs and that leaders emerge or should be assigned to groups on the basis of group needs and not on the basis of the leader's previous experiences, length of service, or general accomplishments. Leaders, in fact, are most effective if they integrate and personify the norms of the group. This really makes the leader the "follower" of the group.

It appears that to gain status and acceptance in a group an individual must conform to the standards of the group upon entering the group. Once this person has demonstrated an acceptance of the group's norms and can make contributions to the group's achievement of goals within these norms, status increases rapidly. Once a high status position is achieved, it is possible to deviate from traditional practices and establish new norms or ways of working.

A most interesting study by Merei conducted some years ago illustrates this point rather well.[2] Children from four to eleven years of age were formed into a dozen homogeneous age groups. Each group met for several sessions until it had institutionalized certain procedures such as seating positions,

---

[2]F. Merei, "Group leadership and institutionalization" in E. Maccoby, T. Newcomb, and E. Hartley (eds.), *Readings in Social Psychology* (3rd edition). New York: Holt, Rinehart & Winston, 1958, pp. 522-532.

permanent division of toys, ceremonies connected with group play, sequences of games, and so forth. Then a leader of about the same age was put into the group. These leaders had been selected on the basis of their status in previous groups. Generally the new leader tried to do away with group traditions and show it new ones. The leader was rejected by the group but quickly made an about face, accepted the group's traditions, and quickly learned considerable skills in them. At this point the new leader was able to introduce modifications into established traditions and gradually introduce new ways of working into the group. Although the new leaders had previously demonstrated more competence than any of their group members, they had to accept and personify the traditions of the group before they gained enough power to start to modify them. Clearly, leaders depend on the group for their power.

There is little possibility of a person influencing a group without being influenced by it or of directing it towards an end not accepted by the members. The leader is interdependent with the other members, and before the members will be influenced by the leader, he or she must demonstrate an acceptance of group norms and traditions. The chief exception is when the leader derives considerable power from outside the group and may be able to coerce members toward unacceptable objectives. The assumptions that leadership is a function of the group and that the group's norms control everyone including the leader help to explain why many groups change very little when a new leader takes over.

LEADERSHIP STYLE

The collapse of the "great man" and trait theories of leadership gave rise to the assumption that leaders were made and not born. As this idea was developed further there became a surge of activity to investigate how people developed certain leadership styles and what impact these styles had on other people—group members, workers, students, and family members. The focus of the first studies were on the authoritarian personality and comparisons of authoritarian and democratic leadership. Following the Ohio State studies and the emergence of goal achievement and group maintenance as the two major dimensions of leadership, they became the focus for examining leadership style. The focus on leadership style comparing or combining goal achievement and group-building orientations represents the state of the art today. Let's examine these orientations and assess the usefulness of their implications for increasing our ability to make groups more effective.

Autocratic-Democratic Styles of Leadership

Leadership styles in this orientation were seen as ranging on a continuum from democratic at one end to autocratic at the other end. But generally leaders were seen as being one or the other and most studies compared democratic and autocratic styles.

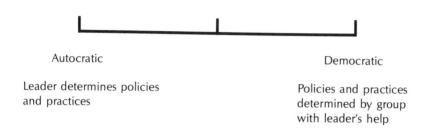

Autocratic   Democratic

Leader determines policies   Policies and practices
and practices   determined by group
                                                            with leader's help

One of the now classical studies in group leadership describes the effects of authoritarian and democratic leadership on the behavior of club members.[3] Small groups of ten-year-old boys were formed to work on theatrical mask making and other projects after school hours. In the first experiment there were two clubs and Lippitt led both, one in a dominating fashion and the other in a participative way. In the follow-up experiment four groups were formed and each one had a dominating and a participative leader for six-week periods. An attempt was made to equate the groups on a number of variables at the time of formation and the groups experienced the style of leadership in a different order to minimize further variables. Also, the team of adults took turns playing dominating and participative leaders to ensure that differences in the boys' recreations were due to the method of leadership and not the personality of the leader.

In the authoritarian clubs all policy was determined by the leader. He dictated the steps of each activity and controlled the task of each member. He was personal in praise or criticism of the work of each member but remained aloof from group participation. He gave direct orders, a number of disrupting commands, and nonconstructive criticism.

---

[3]Ralph White and Ronald Lippitt. *Autocracy and Democracy*. New York: Harper, 1960.

The participative leaders left decisions about group activities up to the total group but guided and assisted them in making a group decision. They outlined general steps to reach their goal and suggested alternative procedures. They participated in the group activity and were objective or helpful in their praise or criticism.

This experiment showed that the boys reacted toward each other in the same way the leader acted toward them. In groups that had an autocratic leader the members were more dominating and aggressive toward each other than in the participative groups. When the leader left the room the participative groups went right on working while the dominated clubs stopped work and fought to see who would replace the leader as authority figure. The children's behavior and attitudes, as well as the extent to which they liked the club, were very closely related to the type of leadership.

In the participative clubs the members were more cooperative and behavior was more constructive. There was more interaction, friendliness, individuality, and creativeness, as well as high group cohesiveness. Hostility was thirty times as frequent in autocratic groups and members were more demanding and discontented. There was also more scapegoating of members and more dropped out of the clubs. Nine-tenths of the boys liked their dominating leader less than the participative leader. On the positive side the autocratic groups produced a bit more in terms of completed projects and had less out-of-field conversation (the price participative groups paid for individuality and freedom).

The second round of this classical study included a third leadership style where there was complete freedom for group or individual decisions and the leader was essentially a complete nonparticipant. This style was named laissez-faire and it was not clear where on the autocratic-democratic continuum it should be placed. Some thought it best to change the straight line into a triangle like this.

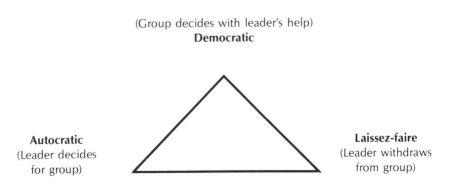

(Group decides with leader's help)
Democratic

Autocratic
(Leader decides
for group)

Laissez-faire
(Leader withdraws
from group)

Most of the following studies continued to contrast democratic with autocratic leadership styles. However, as the terms autocratic and democratic had political overtones and a very heavy value judgment (autocratic was all bad and democratic all good) they were replaced with terms such as dominating and shared leadership or directive and participative leadership.

Studies in classrooms showed that dominating teachers had a high proportion of unproductive behavior in their classrooms and students were more self-centered, frustrated, hostile, and socially negative. In participative classrooms, the teachers were more relaxed and permissive, and there was more friendly, cooperative, socially constructive, and healthy behavior from students. Although dominating teachers often had students who learned as much as or more than less dominated students, the participative teachers found greater changes in their students' attitudes and behavior, more growth in self-direction and confidence, and all-around healthier students.

The same general findings were substantiated in business and industry where supervisors who operated in a participative style, sharing responsibility and decision-making with their subordinates, had high production and good morale (low absenteeism and turnover). While recent studies indicate that production is not always higher under participative supervisors, there is still a strong value judgment that participative leadership is most desirable. This feeling has been encouraged by the quality of working life projects, in which the self-esteem of the worker receives considerable attention, and by the Japanese quality work circles and theory Z management styles.

The leadership style of parents has also been found to be a definite influence on children's behavior and development. Participative-oriented parents have children who tend to be more stable emotionally, more creative, and better adjusted socially than do authoritarian parents. Autocratic parents have been linked to rigid conformity in their children and hostile feelings toward people in general.

Participative Leadership

The same group of people will behave in different ways when the leadership style of the appointed leader changes. And the effectiveness of the group is closely related to the appropriateness of the leader's style to the group's situation. While the participative style has been found to work well in many situations it is not always the most satisfactory. Directive leadership is effective in reaching high production goals in certain situations, is required in emergency situations, and found to be very expediating when people are working well and have a high level of trust. It is also expected when the task is straightforward and the leader is given responsibility for directing action such as the pilot in an airliner or the surgeon in an operating room. Participative leadership by sharing decision making and other responsibilities enables a group to make full use of all its members' potentials and increases self-esteem in the process. This is particularly important in restrictive work situations where jobs are dull and repetitive.

The early studies of participative leadership showed it was a powerful factor in promoting personality development and personal growth in group situations. At that time (1959) I was very involved in training workers in the human service professions and I set out to develop a tool or procedure that would identify participative-oriented leaders. With such a tool it would be possible to see if participative leaders would do better in their work with groups than more autocratic leaders. If the leaders the tool identified as participative were more successful then the same tool could be used to assess the modification of leadership styles through training and supervisory programs.

A wide variety of approaches to identifying participative-oriented leaders were tried out[4] but the most successful was a pencil-and-paper attitude survey. It included some questions from the studies identifying the authoritarian personality, a cooperation scale from the Guilford-Zimmerman Temperament Survey, and some questions about leadership beliefs. The Dimock Leadership Inventory[5] emerged and was found to measure a flexible, cooperative, participative orientation to working with others. It was

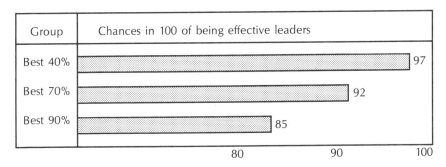

Selecting Group Leaders with the Dimock Leadership Inventory

Group	Chances in 100 of being effective leaders
Best 40%	97
Best 70%	92
Best 90%	85

80   90   100

---

[4]These approaches and their results are described in H. G. Dimock, "Selecting and Training Group Leaders" Report No. 13. Montreal: Centre for Human Relations and Community Studies, Concordia University, 1970.

[5]Sheridan Psychological Services, Box 6101, Orange, California 92667 (1970).

validated on three hundred and fifty people working in fifteen small-group leadership situations such as youth groups and summer camps. All the leaders completed the inventory in advance of their jobs and scores were correlated with on-the-job ratings given to them by their supervisor as part of a performance appraisal. While the results decisively illustrated that participative-oriented leaders were more successful as rated by their supervisors, it was not a continuous correlation. That is, the most participative leaders were not any better than the moderately participative leaders, but the authoritarian-oriented leaders were not successful, and this was true more than nine times out of ten.

A few years after developing the Leadership Inventory, I used it to check the studies that showed students in participative-led classrooms changed their attitudes and beliefs most. Thirty-one university classes, leadership training programs, and supervisory situations were studied with over nine hundred participants. The programs were divided into four categories based on the degree to which learners participated in the situation. All groups were rated on the amount of change the participants showed on the Dimock Leadership Inventory: no change, some change, or considerable change. The results shown below confirmed the previous research that concluded that participating in a learning experience facilitated a change in attitudes toward those found to be associated with on-the-job success.[6] Again these studies showed that there was more attitude change from the low participation groups compared to the medium participation groups than from the medium participation to the very high participation groups. It seems learning does not increase as participation increases, but that a shift from nonparticipation to participation generates a significant increase. These findings of an optimum in participative leadership could be important as they would explain why the high participation orientations of humanistic education, child-centered parenting, and self-actualizing therapy and personal growth groups have not improved on the results of more moderate participation.

Participation and Attitude Change Measured on the Dimock Leadership Inventory

	Low N = 4	Medium N = 6	High N =12	Very High N =9
Amount of Change	None = 4 Some = 0 A Lot = 0	None = 2 Some = 3 A Lot = 1	None = 1 Some = 6 A Lot = 5	None = 1 Some = 4 A Lot = 4

[6]H. G. Dimock, "Sensitivity training as a method of increasing on-the-job effectiveness," *Sociological Inquiry*, 41: 227-231, 1971.

Goal Achievement
and Group-Building Leadership Styles

The identification of two major dimensions of leadership in the Ohio State studies led to the development of two-dimensional leadership theories (the autocratic-democratic theory was one dimension) incorporating goal achievement orientation and group building/maintenance. These functional leadership theories saw leaders and, in fact, all group members assessed on their orientation or concern for goal achievement (also called task accomplishment or concern for production) and group building/maintenance (also called concern for people or relationships).

Thus, we first look at how much concern or motivation a person has toward task accomplishment, and how much toward group building/maintenance. Suppose a person had been rated as follows:

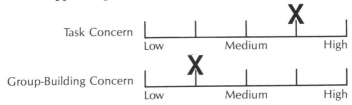

These ratings would now be combined on a two-dimensional matrix and general descriptions applied as shown in Figure 1.

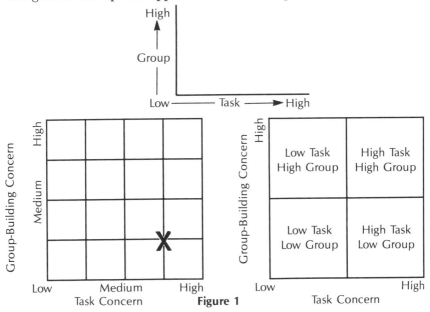

Figure 1

The person so rated would now be described as a high task, low group-building leader. Generally, this leadership theory, as personified by the Blake Grid,[7] assumed that there was a best leadership style and that it was a high task, high group-building style, which had been supported by the Ohio State and related research.[8] The one best style of leadership did not integrate well with the studies showing that leadership was a function of situational variables, and new situational theories developed.

Theories of Leadership as a Function of the Situation

In several theories, leadership is seen as a function of the situation. As the factors in the situation change, it is anticipated that different styles of leadership will be most effective. Thus, one of the vital variables in the success of a group is the appropriateness of the leader's style to the situation. In considering this match between the leadership style and the situation, these theories propose that it is the situation that should determine the style. Or, as we said earlier, it is the followers that set the scene and expectations for the leader.

The most useful of the situational theories adds a third dimension to our previous two of goal achievement and group building, and it assesses the appropriateness of the style on these two dimensions for the situation.

The important implication of the addition of this situational appropriateness dimension is no one best leadership style remains, as the effectiveness of the style varies with the situation. Thus, in some situations a high task style will be best while at other times a high group-building style will be most appropriate. The development of these theories by Reddin,[9] Hersey and Blanchard (1977), and Fiedler (1974) clarifies that leaders can increase their effectiveness by enlarging their repertoire of leadership styles and by not being confined to the same style as the needs and situations change. Moreover, by developing their skills in diagnosing the situations they are working in, leaders can make better choices of the appropriate style to use. As a leader becomes more flexible and comfortable in using a variety of leadership styles and becomes more competent in diagnosing leadership situations and plugging in the most approriate style, that leader's effectiveness will increase. Let's see how it works.

---

[7]R. Blake and J. Mouton, "How to choose a leadership style," *Training and Development Journal*, pp. 39-47, February, 1982.

[8]Robert Blake and Jane Mouton, *The Managerial Grid*. Houston: Gulf, 1964.

[9]William Reddin, *Managerial Effectiveness*. New York: McGraw-Hill, 1970.

We have the two dimensions of goal achievement (which we'll call TASK for task accomplishment), and group building/maintenance (which we'll shorten to GROUP). These are combined into a two-dimensional form as shown in Figure 2. The form is divided for convenience into four squares representing four major combinations of the two dimensions and proposing four major leadership styles. Giving these four styles names will make it easier to talk about them.

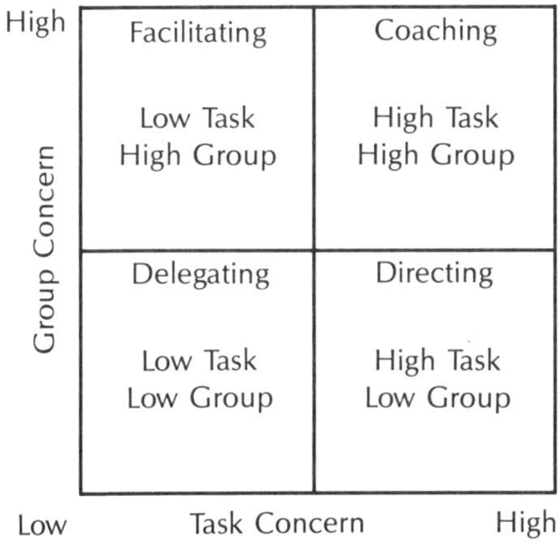

High	Facilitating	Coaching
	Low Task High Group	High Task High Group
	Delegating	Directing
	Low Task Low Group	High Task Low Group
Low	Task Concern	High

(Group Concern on vertical axis; Task Concern on horizontal axis)

Figure 2

Most leaders have a style that they prefer to use and in the hundreds of human service staff groups with whom I've worked it is a coaching style (high task, high group). Some staff typically use a directing style and others use a facilitating style but very few in my studies prefer the delegating style. All four styles can be equally useful as each of the four is most effective in certain situations. The well-rounded leader would ideally be equally comfortable and skillful in each of the four basic styles.

Directing. Initiating and providing structure (how and when things will be done), providing clear directions about what is to be done and expectations about quantity and quality (defining roles and expectations), providing information about the environment or organization within which the group operates, evaluating and monitoring task accomplishment, and generally emphasizing goal achievement.

Coaching. Continues to provide much of the structure, task emphasis, and monitoring/evaluating functions of the directing style but does so as a coach rather than a boss. Additional roles are providing support and encouragement, showing personal interest in members' well-being, seeking more reaction and feedback from members, and generally establishing a supportive, personal relationship with followers.

Facilitating. Involves followers in making the decisions that affect them and facilitates their problem-solving and decision-making activities, provides social/emotional support, coordinates group activities, mediates and harmonizes interpersonal problems, builds strong, cohesive relationships within group, and generally builds harmonious, personally enhancing relationships with followers.

Delegating. Delegating responsibility and accountability to followers and then letting them do it, giving recognition for noteworthy accomplishments, protecting members from outside trivia and liaisoning with related groups or parts of the organization on followers' behalf, and generally demonstrating trust and confidence in followers' ability to accomplish the task and maintain themselves as a healthy, viable group.

The Effectiveness Dimension

Establishing which of these four styles is likely to be the most appropriate depends on an accurate diagnosis of the situation at a given time. I say at a given time because a group that has worked together for some time may experience different needs and pressures as new members join the group, it moves to a new location, its budget is cut or expanded, or other groups move in to compete with the programs they provide.

In assessing situational factors there are no hard and fast rules but several factors continually emerge. Generally the focus is on the *followers* and the *situation*. They are assessed on a poor-fair-good continuum.

Followers

An accurate assessment of a group's followers would include: competence of the members to accomplish the tasks or performance/knowledge skills, motivation to accomplish the tasks, previous experience or training with the task, and self-confidence in accomplishing the task. (Rate these items as poor, fair, or good.)

Situation

An accurate assessment of a group's situation would include: clarity of the task and how to accomplish it; general understanding of the environment, the usual ways of working, and expectations for group members; the personal power (how much the followers prefer and like the leader) and position power (ability to reward and punish the members) of the leader; and the quality of interpersonal relations within the group. (Rate these factors as poor, fair, or good.) Figure 3 shows the style most likely to be effective given the rating of the situational factors.

Summary

Leaders will benefit from diagnosing the situational factors at a given time in the groups where they are providing leadership. As these factors move assessments from poor to fair they will increase their group-building functions and shift their styles from one of directing to coaching and then to

Appropriate Leadership Style As Situational Factors
Move from Poor to Good

Figure 3

facilitating. As the situational factors move to good it may be appropriate to move to a delegating style or if the group is asking for direction and action, a directing style. Groups that "have it all together" may prefer to "run their own show" without a lot of over-the-shoulder help from the leader. Or they may prefer some direct action taking and assignment of specific tasks as they trust the leader and want to eliminate lengthy planning meetings as they get on with the task to which they are all committed.

Some Implications

1. Starting a new group with the successful accomplishment of a task can be helpful. For many years my style was to start a new group in a facilitating style, helping people to get to know one another and work out the ways they wanted to proceed with meeting their task accomplishment expectations. Figure 3 (the model) suggests that this is appropriate for groups where the situational factors are fair but not where the factors are poor. As it is always best to start on the right side of the model (it is easier to give social/emotional rewards and status to participants than to take them away), I now start with high structure and direction while I assess the situational factors and then move to coaching and facilitating as quickly as these factors indicate.

2. Moving from one style to another should be done slowly and without skipping a style. It was my practice to provide an extensive orientation for new staff or students who reported to me (directing) but after they knew the job or course and its expectations, I moved to a delegating style. This model helped me to understand why I needed to move into a coaching style, and then a facilitating style before leaving them to "sink or swim." As a colleague of mine often says, "Moving quickly from a directing style to a delgating style keeps the jails full."

3. These understandings help to focus on the alternative actions leaders should consider when their efforts to be helpful are not working well. It may highlight that a leader has difficulty providing the structure and direction a new group of relatively unskilled people needs (which may be why many people prefer working with older youth rather than with young children).

4. As the model is a developmental one, and since we expect that groups and individuals will grow and develop from poor situational factors to good situational factors, it focuses on the style the leader should be moving toward as the leader encourages this growth. Many leaders find it difficult to move from a coaching style to a facilitating style as it means

giving up control. This is illustrated in many families where the greatest tension comes when adolescents are ready for a facilitating (low task, high group) style but parents tend to remain in a coaching style that continues to monitor and evaluate activities and performance.

5. This also helps to explain why some leaders "rise to their level of incompetence" in an organization. A swimming pool instructor established a fine record of successes and was promoted to aquatics director for the agency. In her role of instructor she used her usual leadership style of high task with some group building which was exactly what the situation called for. But as team leader of the aquatics staff where the situational factors (staff competence and motivation, group solidarity) were fair, the high task approach was no longer successful. The staff resented the constant monitoring of their work and constant pressure, morale sank, and there were frequent complaints from staff moving through the agency. With a poor record as aquatics director, it is unlikely she would be considered for a promotion, and hence she would stay on in the aquatics position having "risen to her level of incompetence."

6. Following up from the above example, it is evident that the followers and situation determine the appropriate leadership style. This should encourage us as leaders to diagnose these situational factors in a new job and if they don't fit our usual leadership style, consider whether we are prepared to change our style or should turn down the appointment to that situation. And, as supervisors, we could consider the situational factors as part of selecting the most appropriate person for an assignmnent or new position. The supervisor of the aquatics instructor could be faulted for not being more aware of the likely inappropriateness of her usual style and of not providing the directing and coaching to help her make the transition.

LEADERSHIP SUMMARY

While leaders have some traits or characteristics that differentiate them from followers, these characteristics are not very important in understanding leadership and are usually related to the situation in which the leadership takes place. Leadership is best thought of as a group function where most members will be contributing to the achievement of group goals and to the maintenance and growth of the group. Depending on the situational factors, different styles of leadership or amounts of task achievement and group-building behaviors will be most appropriate. Diagnosing the quality of these situational factors can help in selecting the leadership style (or leader) most likely to be effective in that situation.[10] Leaders can increase their effectiveness by enlarging their repertoire of task and group-building skills, and by sharpening their diagnostic skills.

---

[10]Diagnostic tools and methods are presented in Part 2, How to Observe Your Group.

Chapter 2

Understanding Group Structure

The preceding chapter on leadership concluded that there were two major ways leaders could increase their effectiveness: enlarging their repertoire of task and group-building behaviors and improving their group diagnosis skills. Countless studies on the outcomes of leadership training have not been encouraging. While it seems possible to help leaders develop additional task and group-building skills, this has had little impact on modifying the leaders' preferred or basic leadership style. Yet in recent years there have been hundreds of leadership training programs and hardly a program on group diagnostic skills.

People who come together in groups tend to form structures and develop standards that help them to operate effectively and maintain themselves as a group. These standards or "usual ways of doing things" are most helpful to the group as everyone knows what is going to happen and how it is going to happen. These clear-cut procedures or ways of doing things are evident in parliament, church services, camp programs, and nursing team report sessions. These "usual ways of doing things" are often called the culture of the group or organization. Members are expected to conform to these standards or informal rules and pressure is often exerted by the group on individuals who deviate from them. From this process of social control a group derives its strength to pull together as a group and increase its effectiveness and morale.

A group or team is more than the sum of its parts—it is a social system with its own structure and culture. Once a structure and culture are established, they may be fairly difficult to change and studies have shown it is often easier to start up a new group than to get an existing group to change. Members may come and go in a group but as the culture belongs to the group as a whole, it stays put. Only by changing a "critical mass" of the members at one time is there a fair chance that the usual ways of doing things might also change.

There are two sources of norms and standards in most groups: those that originate from the organization (recreation center, school, hospital, community agency) and those that are established informally by the group. A good example of external and internal norms at work can usually be found around meeting times or work hours. The external norm is that the meeting will start at 7:30 p.m. or the working day at 9:00 a.m., yet members usually know what time it will really start or when other people will arrive. In one organization with which I was associated the work day started at 9:00 and people usually arrived about then but took fifteen or twenty minutes to get and drink coffee. In a sense they met the external norm by being on time yet the informal norm was that actual work started twenty to thirty minutes later.

These norms mobilize powerful forces that influence the behavior of members and determine the outcome of many organizational goals. Understanding and working with these norms can provide the essential element that is often missing in our work with groups, whether it be team teaching and open classrooms in education, coaching a team, leading a quality circle in industry, or working on a community rehabilitation program. Also, these norms, along with the technical skills and competence of the members, determine what will be the most effective leadership style for that group. And, if changes are to be made in the way the group is working, these norms will have to change.

GROUP MEMBERSHIP

All individuals have the same basic needs for love, security, recognition, a sense of accomplishment, and power. Most of these needs, like other physical, educational, and spiritual needs in our society, are satisfied through relationships with other individuals or groups of individuals. Generally, people try to find relationships or groups in which these needs can be met. Individuals are attracted to groups that appear to be able to meet their needs; hence, in any group situation members are looking for ways to satisfy their needs.

Members who form a group on a voluntary basis, such as an after-school team or club, are more likely to find satisfaction and be attracted to the group than members who are not free to come and go, such as in a school class. My father found in his studies that voluntary groups had more solidarity and influence on member behavior than groups with nonvoluntary members. Procedures or activities that increase the satisfaction of member needs usually increase the group's solidarity, too.

The specific attraction to a particular group may be based on personal attraction to the other members, the nature of the group goals or tasks, or the prestige of the group in the eyes of other people. People may find satisfaction in a group because the members like them and make them feel secure. Or the activity of the group, such as a team sport, singing, craft work, or skiing, may provide an opportunity for them to gain considerable recognition if they excel in that skill. A group taking on worthwhile community service projects can provide a real sense of accomplishment for its members. Sometimes people seek membership in a group that has high prestige in the community hoping it will give them more acceptance or perhaps open up contacts for furthering business and professional interests.

Physical location is another factor affecting attraction to a group and membership. Studies of Y's and Boys' and Girls' Clubs have shown that most members come from within a mile radius of the building. Joining adult education courses is related to what is offered locally. Informal groups in the community, such as bridge clubs and Sunday hockey players, tend to be composed of people who live close to one another. And in work situations, informal groups often reflect the physical proximity of the members.

Recognizing the reasons members join a group and then helping to satisfy these reasons is a powerful way of building strong, healthy groups. Probably the most common misconception I've found in this regard is that leaders assume members have joined their groups because of the content of their activity, such as a glee club, ceramics group, or Shakespeare class. In reality members joined for social reasons, and the activity simply provided a vehicle and a legitimization for getting together.

FACTORS CONTRIBUTING TO STRONG GROUPS

The strength or solidarity of a group is determined chiefly by the personal need satisfaction it provides members or by the expectation of that need satisfaction. Solidarity and cohesion increase as the group becomes more attractive to the members and there is an increased interest in taking part in its programs. The more members are attracted to a group because of what it can or does offer them the higher will be its cohesion. An individual who is lured to a group on the promise of exciting activities and personal rewards will not continue to be attracted to the group if it does not live up to expectations or in other ways provide personal satisfaction. The basis of a group's solidarity often determines how members will react in a group. If the basis of attraction to the group is the personal relations with other members, then meetings are likely to be warm and friendly with perhaps only moderate interest in planning and decision making related to tasks. This appeared to be the case in a community development study a few years ago. The core planning group was made up of young homemakers who enjoyed their personal relations, and though they were interested in the community project, it was not the basis of attraction to the group. The formal planning session with a chairperson, agenda, and minutes did not meet their needs, so we instituted a meeting after the meeting that was unstructured, and people talked about what they were feeling during the meeting or about what was going on in their lives.

Another factor contributing to group strength is the size of the group. Other things being equal, smaller groups are more cohesive than larger groups. In a small group (five to thirteen members) there is more interaction among members, and increased interaction tends to increase positive feelings among members, which, in turn, increases attraction for the group. The increased participation possible for each member in a small group also promotes satisfaction. Geographical location and physical proximity also tend to increase interaction and thus can be other contributors to group strength.

Leadership style has a considerable impact on solidarity with facilitating, participative-oriented leadership encouraging interaction and relationship building. Certainly the more that members participate in making the decisions which affect them, have a clear picture of the goals of the group, and a recognized part to play in helping the group reach those goals, the higher will be the group's cohesion. Coaching and facilitative leaders also help members get recognition and self-enhancement as the group goes about its work and this increases attraction to the group. Showing concern for members' well-being is consistently related to group cohesion. Task-oriented styles can contribute to group strength by increasing satisfaction with concrete accomplishments and especially by helping members clarify their expectations of the group. Permissive and laissez-faire styles have no pattern of relationship to group cohesion.

Groups where members are working toward a common goal on a cooperative basis are usually more cohesive than groups in which the members are in competition with one another. Competition with an outside group, however, can have a powerful influence in expanding a group's solidarity. This understanding is frequently used by sales managers, team leaders, schoolteachers, and even governments as they seek an outside group to "fight" against, expecting the competition to pull the group together and increase task accomplishment in the process. While competition does tend to increase cohesion it is not without detriment to the group as leadership usually centralizes and becomes more directive, tension rises, and aggression and scapegoating increase.

Working with an outside group on a vital task that requires the full participation of members of both groups is about as powerful an influence on cohesion as competition. This approach also increases cohesion without harmful side effects on the group. Interest in win-win games, activities, and projects has demonstrated useful alternatives to traditional win-lose activities, and the swing in this direction will increase as the range and quality of activities continue to expand.

Anything that helps a group to feel special or unique can contribute to group strength, such as a name, insignia, pennant, special meeting room, unique stationery, initiation rituals, and regular ceremonies. Many groups have special songs or cheers that add to group spirit. In Japan some work groups start the day with a company song followed by a traditional set of physical exercises. And probably the biggest winner along this line is some sort of distinguishing costume. IBM has its three-piece suits and white shirts, youth groups have their jeans and jogging shoes, and street gangs have their "all the same" jackets. Organizations can also contribute to the solidarity of their groups by playing up their importance to the community, by the kind of public support and financial assistance they receive (or give), by their national or international status, or by anything else that might increase the attractiveness of their groups.

There is some support for the assumption that the difficulty of getting into a group increases attraction for members. People often want most those things which are hard to get while easy things are taken for granted. If people work hard to qualify for group membership it is expected that they will value that membership more highly than otherwise. Asking too little of group members loses more members than asking for a high but attainable contribution.

New groups usually set very high and quite optimistic goals. And, groups that are working toward a clear set of overall goals tend to prefer more difficult short-term goals to easy ones. Group goals can be increased after both success and failure and may become unattainable. The frustration and disappointment this can generate may reduce the group's attractiveness and thus its cohesion. High but attainable goals are encouraged by frequent reports on results to provide comparisons and a realistic basis for setting new goals.

Cohesion is the glue that holds groups together and if factors inside or outside the group start to decrease this cohesion, the group will begin to fall apart. If action is not taken to reverse this trend there will be disorganization and collapse, and if the group is a voluntary one, the members will go their separate ways. Members will leave a voluntary group at the point where the forces attracting them to the group are equal to or outnumbered by the forces pulling them away form the group. We might say that when the net attractiveness of a group is zero or a negative amount, its members will start leaving. While attractiveness dimensions vary from member to member the net attractiveness is often similar and when this point is reached usually several members will leave at the same time (especially if part of their attraction was to each other). A high turnover in membership is usually a pretty accurate symptom of an unhealthy group. Some groups with poor group strength can be lost for several years with the members in an apathetic state simply because the groups have become institutionalized and the members continue to come as part of a routine or in memory of other days.

In summing up, I'd like to highlight that, for a group to be strong, members must be attracted to the group, be clear about their role in the group and how they can contribute to achieving the group's goals, and be integrated into the group's standards and norms. Groups function most effectively when members agree on goals, standards, and usual ways of doing things. These in turn help each of the members to know what is expected of them, how they can behave most appropriately and get recognition and approval, what they can expect from their colleagues, and how the group is likely to meet their personal and professional needs. In a cohesive group members want their group to succeed so they can continue to find the satisfactions that attracted them to the group, and, as it continues to succeed, members glow with pride and satisfaction about their efforts. An identity and recognition as a separate group, high but attainable goals, optimal interaction and proximity, and facilitative leadership that encourages participation in decision making and member well-being help build a cohesive group.

GROUP STANDARDS AND SOCIAL CONTROL

The cohesion of a group is the glue that holds it together and makes it click. Cohesion—the sum of members' attraction to the group—provides the power to motivate members to abide by a group's standards and usual ways of working. Without solidarity there is little group influence over members' behavior and unless the group has some coercive power available (such as in schools and many work places), the group can end up a collection of individuals all doing their own things. As a group develops standards about what is acceptable member behavior it also develops forces which put pressure on members to conform to these standards. The more members are attracted to the group and want to see it succeed, the stronger are the forces likely to be. An understanding of group standards and the forces supporting can help to explain what is going on in a group and why some groups are successful and some are not. Guiding these forces can be an important contribution of the group worker to the value of the experience for the members.

Healthy groups encourage the *conformity* of members to group standards, but this does not mean *uniformity of behavior.* Standards of healthy groups may encourage all members to make their unique contributions to the group—that is, people should be themselves as much as possible. Or, the expectations for participants may be that they will work in cooperative, interdependent ways; participate in consensual decision-making processes; and express any differences they feel so the group can consider all alternatives. In these groups, individuals who think and feel differently from the group (the creative minority) are supported by the group's standards for their differences as long as they also conform to working in cooperative, interdependent ways around the differences. Having members conform by expressing similar opinions or all acting the same does not usually help a group. But having members conform to a standard of sticking together to try to work out differences, to find decisions that will be tolerable to all, is most desirable.

Uniformity of behavior where members are expected to think, dress, and act alike is usually found in groups that are immature, anxious or frightened, or under considerable pressure from outside the group. To these groups of insecure members, having everyone "talk the same" appears to protect the group against these fears. While the *uniformity* and "sheep-like" behavior of members is a real concern in a freedom-loving, humanistic society, it is usually a symptom of scared, pressured, or immature groups. Helping to develop strong, healthy groups reduces the need for restrictive group standards based on uniformity of behavior. Let's put our energies into working on the problem, not railing about the symptoms.

The function of social pressures on members to conform to group standards is to help facilitate and organize the accomplishment of group goals and maintain the group as a functioning social system. To have a successful meeting, for instance, a group needs most of its members to be there and at about the same time (or the ones who come early may get frustrated and leave). Some kind of a standard with some pressure to abide by the standard is useful to group members. The pressure can take the form of a "you're late again" comment, a fine, an extra duty, or all the way up to a dismissal from the group. Some time ago I read about a high school basketball team that was hell bent on winning all its games. The team set up rigid rules for training and practice, which were strictly enforced. Players breaking the ten o'clock curfew were brought before the team and "pressured" back into line. Missing practice or breaking curfew more than once could result in being drubbed out of the team.

The more members are attracted to a group and internalize its goals, the more likely they are to abide by the group's standards and to press one another to do so. This social control helps the group to work expediently and greatly increases the satisfaction of participants with the group. This, in turn, helps to increase the group's solidarity. This is a circular phenomena as the more cohesive a group is, the more it can exert social pressure; the more it can exert pressure on members to conform to its standards, the greater will be the members' satisfaction; and the greater the satisfaction of members with the group, the higher will be its cohesion.

THE POWER OF GROUP PRESSURE

The power of group pressure has been frequently illustrated in laboratory experiments where individuals were pressured by others into an opinion or behavior which was against their better judgment (Hare, 1976). In one classical study a naive subject was shown a small ray of light in a dark room and asked to estimate the distance of its movement. It was very difficult to tell if the light was moving or not as there were no reference points, but when a subject was joined by others who were in on the experiment and pretended they saw the light moving (it did not move), the naive subject started making similar estimates. Most subjects were heavily influenced by the other members' opinions.

In another study subjects were asked to match the length of a standard line with three comparison lines. The three comparison lines were of quite different lengths, and it was easy to tell which line matched. In order to study the effect on the subjects of majority opinions that appeared contrary to fact, seven other people, who had conspired with the experimenter, were added to form a group. These members gave incorrect answers; and most subjects, when confronted by the incorrect group majority opinion, modified their own judgments. About a third of the subjects distorted their judgments in order to completely agree with the majority.

Cards Used in Experiment on Group Pressure

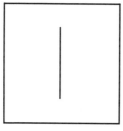

Standard line

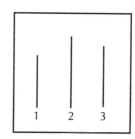

Comparison lines

Another "shocking" experiment (Milgram, Hare, 1976) went even further in studying conformity to authority. The above studies had suggested that if one of the group members in cahoots with the experimenter had some authority status, the naive subject was more likely to accept that person's judgment than other group members. So, in this experiment, the naive subject was directed to administer an electric shock to a victim under the guise of a study of the effects of punishment on memory. Over half of the subjects on the direction of the experimenter administered "dangerous, severe shocks" to the victims (though the victims yelled and screamed on being shocked, it was all faked).

Subjects were more likely to conform to group pressure in the first study where the ray of light presented a vague or ambiguous stimulus than in the second study where the lines had clear parameters. It may be concluded that the more general or ambiguous the topic of discussion is, the more an individual will be influnced by majority opinions. In a group setting a member will more likely conform to group pressure when discussing what life will be like ten years from now than when discussing the legal status of capital punishment.

THE IMPACT OF GROUP PRESSURE

The more participants want to remain in a group, the more likely they are to abide by its standards. And the more members value the standard, see its usefulness, and believe that adhering to that standard will help the group, the more they will support it and pressure other members to do so. A person who deviates from the norms of the group gradually becomes the focus of attention. For example, a woman may be ignored and have nothing said about her conduct, but as that doesn't give a very clear message, the deviant may miss it completely. Similar behavior within a short time span may cause members to talk about her behind her back hoping that the word will get back to her. The next level is usually some kind of side remark said in the person's presence but in a jocular manner. The deviant continues to be isolated from other communication to strengthen the rejection, and additional bad-mouthing bringing up other faults helps to increase the isolation. The final form of group pressure is some kind of direct confrontation by the group or by a member who takes on the role of group enforcer. Some kind of separation or removal from the group may be threatened at that time. In addition to actual removal, a group may withdraw the deviant's privileges (take away a parking space, move her to a smaller office, or take back loaned equipment), give her dead-end assignments, send her on "wild goose chases," or cut her off from notification of future meetings and other important communication.

How deviants will respond to group pressure depends not only on how much they want to stay in the group but how important continuing that behavior is to them. It also depends on how clear and harsh the messages and punishments are, as they may be able to tolerate the snide remarks but find a conspiracy of silence too much to handle. Sometimes a behavior that is found deviant in one group is the accepted standard in another, and the individual is faced with conflicting values. In such cases the deviant will usually stick with the most attractive behavior approved by the group. Parents are shocked when they see their children continuing behavior supported that is in their peer group, but that is in defiance of family standards and parental pressure to conform. For some youths it is more important to have the acceptance of their peer group at a point in time than that of their parents.

People are more likely to conform to a group's standards if it is the most important group in their life or if, at least for a period of time, it is the only group. Without outside reference points and reminders of usual standards the power of the present group increases immensely. The army uses this technique in virtually isolating its new recruits in boot camp. Hospitals do the same when they limit or otherwise discourage outsiders visiting as this increases the adherence of patients to hospital norms. Similar strong pressures develop in communes, monasteries, submarines, and isolated oil rigs or work areas.

This factor has been used in training programs that were trying to increase the impact of the training on group participants. Personal growth groups may be held on a residential basis in a remote area. Nonparticipants (family members or friends) are not allowed and telephones are not readily available (no calls are taken during work sessions). Most activities—eating, sleeping, recreation—are done with other members, thus increasing interaction and group influence potential. Marathon groups intensify this process by meeting for eighteen or twenty hours a day nonstop and then perhaps sleeping in the same room. It is well documented how powerful this isolation from usual activities and reference points can be and how, after a few days, participants are ready to experiment with very new and different behavior. Group leaders work at building group standards that will encourage this freeing up, self-exploration process by setting up group rules, modeling appropriate behavior, and rewarding those who do and perhaps punishing those who don't conform to the standards.

Factors Affecting the Strength of Group Pressures

1. **The effect conformity will have on group success**
   Deviant behavior blocking the group from an important objective will receive more pressure than deviation which is merely annoying and distracting.

2. **The cohesion of the group**
   Cohesive groups have more power to exert strong pressures, and are more likely to use them.

3. **Discrepancy of deviant behavior**
   The wider the divergence of behavior from accepted standards, the greater will be the pressure to conform.

4. **Group status of the deviant**
   Members who are well accepted by the group and are moving up in the system will receive more pressure than "odd balls" who aren't important to the group.

5. **Visibility of the deviation**
   High-visibility deviations such as dress, public statements, and written documents receive more pressure than washroom mutterings.

These are powerful forces that have a significant impact on attitude and behavior change and, while the participants of personal growth groups are paying big money for the opportunity, the same factors make up the pressures used in "brainwashing" where the tools are not voluntarily bought into by the captive and often-coerced participants.

Many everyday groups in social agencies, churches, and schools use some of these factors when they go on a trip together or attend a conference, hold meetings off the job site, go on a retreat, or just schedule in a weekend for intensive work on a particular problem. Increasing physical togetherness, interaction, and isolation can help to maximize the impact of pressures toward group standards.

Groups that are strong and healthy encourage members to think and act creatively, initiate new ideas, and propose different ways of doing things. This allows some deviation from usual ways of doing things and will be tolerated or even encouraged if the deviant is a high-status member of the group and the behavior holds some hope of being useful to the group. At

---

Factors Affecting Conformity to Pressures

1. **Desire to remain part of the group**
   The more a member sees the group as attractive and wants to retain membership, the greater will be the influence of group pressures toward conformity.

2. **The strength, visibility, and clarity of pressures**
   Public humiliation with a comprehensive review of transgressions is more powerful than a few vague unflattering comments in the parking lot.

3. **Conflicts with other group standards**
   If conforming to the standards of one group means breaking the standards of an equally important group in a way that is highly visible, it will be less acceptable than if there is no conflict.

4. **The character of the individual**
   Individuals vary in their proneness to yield to group pressure because of personal factors. People with self-confidence and inner security are least likely to be affected by social pressure.

5. **The certainty of the sanctions**
   Group pressure that leaves no doubt about what will happen as a result of the deviant behavior is most likely to be effective.

---

other times minor infractions of group standards by well-accepted members may be tolerated as others say "There goes Mavis again, off on her hobby horse." Members also earn the right to be different based on their past contribution to the group. If new members complain about their idiosyncrasies, they are told of their previous outstanding services to the group.

GROUP STRUCTURE AND GOALS

The presentation on group structure so far has discussed group membership and what attracts people to groups; factors related to group solidarity; and group standards and social control. To continue the presentation of group standards and norms it is helpful to look at the kind of goals a group has, and how the members interact and make decisions. These dimensions help to round out a picture of a group and provide a fairly comprehensive overview of group structure (Climate, Involvement, Interaction, Cohesion, and Productivity).

Group goals can be rated on the extent to which they encourage members to work together and collaborate, work independently, or compete. Members of boards of directors of the community serving associations with whom I've worked usually see themselves working toward a common goal and collaboration as helping to achieve their goals. When I was a member of a swimming team we worked toward a common goal (being conference champions) but winning depended on the skills of individual members. As a consultant to a large insurance company I found the salespeople and managers in competition with one another over the volume of sales. The differences in these goals typically influence group structure. Groups with goals achieved through collaboration develop standards related to the quality of the group's performance. Members become more concerned about what happens to the group's performance than about their own performance. This often results in more cohesion, more interaction, and more pressures for members to conform to group standards. If members participate in establishing the group's goal, their commitment to it as well as their readiness to abide by group standards and encourage others to do so, increases. This increased motivation for group success and thus the attractiveness of the group builds group solidarity. As members' desire for group success increases, so do efforts to achieve that success.

During an extensive study of over a thousand recreation workers (Dimock, 1979) I found that there were two types of groups the recreation workers led: goals achieved through member collaboration groups; and goals achieved through individual successes groups. In the latter category are figure skating, swimming, skiing, gymnastics, boxing, and similar individual sport or activity groups. The relationships of the members in the groups were different, and in individual activity groups the staff used coaching styles of leadership while in the other groups the facilitating style was more appropriate. The concept of superordinate goals is that when the goals can only be accomplished by all the members of one or more groups working together, it becomes a powerful unifying force. Group motivation is most likely to develop when the group's accomplishments can be attributed to the effort of the group as a whole rather than to individual members.

STATUS AND POSITION

Norms and structure provide order for the group and help to coordinate and focus individual behavior. Knowing who gets to do what, and what the expectations are for each member is an important part of a group working smoothly with a high level of satisfaction for the members. To help clarify structure, groups develop a status or position hierarchy. The position hierarchy is based on assigned positions such as president, vice president, team leader, and chairperson, and may or may not be related to competence and popularity. But these positions are clearly visible and usually the power, privileges, and responsibilities that go with the position are pretty well defined.

There is another equally important hierarchy that is based on personal status and although it is rarely discussed it exists in a definite form. Personal status is what people earn in their relationships with others and in their skills and abilities to help the group with its products. A street gang may base its status hierarchy on toughness, a board of directors on financial resources, and a work group on concern for others. More usually, there is a variety of factors determining to whom a group will assign personal status.

In the rural area we call this hierarchy a "gate order" as it describes cows coming into the barn from the field. As milking time approaches the cows bunch up at the gate, blocking the entrance into the barn. Once the gate is opened the cows file quickly through and always in the same gate order. Imagine the confusion and shoving if the cows did not know what the gate order was and where their position occurred.

The status hierarchy in groups of people performs much the same function of organization and coordination. However, as humans don't "line up" and demonstrate the order as clearly as cows, people have to refine their observation skills to pick it up. Groups with clearly established hierarchies— where all participants know what is expected of them and what they can expect from each other—function more satisfactorily than groups where it remains vague. In new groups much of the early activity can be best understood as members are trying to work out their hierarchy and are "jockeying for position" in the process. Accuracy in perceiving the status positions of others is closely associated with status as the members who can't put it together usually don't know what is going on in the group or where they stand with other people, and this decreases their usefulness and prestige.

DECISION-MAKING STRUCTURES

Closely related to the question of who has power in the group as illustrated by a status hierachy is the question of "who gets to decide what for whom." There are two parts to this question that are important to the group as both of them affect cohesion and member satisfaction. First, we should check on how clear and consistent the deciding processes are, for the clearer they are the greater will be their potential usefulness. And, second, the procedures used will also influence cohesion and motivation as the more members join in establishing group goals, and see them as appropriate and attainable, the higher will be the cohesion and member readiness to work on these goals.

The clarity of the structure, irrespective of how appropriate the structure is to the needs of the group, is important. Structures that are clear can be changed while it is much harder to deal with vague structures. Some leaders and managers seem to recognize this intuitively and keep the structures vague and constantly changing so as to retain their power and control by avoiding input or confrontation from others. Structures that become too specific can be very restrictive and I am sure that *Robert's Rules of Order* has hindered more groups than it has helped. Inconsistencies in structures or procedures are extremely frustrating and many are the times I have heard children, students, and workers say, "If only they would be consistent, I wouldn't mind so much what they *did.*" Ideally we would choose norms and structures that continually develop and evolve through the participation of group members so that they can make the optimal contributions to the group.

FREQUENTLY ASKED QUESTIONS

A frequently asked and extensively studied question is, "Does increasing cohesion increase productivity?" The book is still open on this question as it does not appear that there is any consistent pattern. It is clear, however, that increasing cohesion increases member satisfaction with the group. But this is not a big surprise as cohesion is defined as the sum of members' attraction to the group.

"Are individuals or groups more effective in accomplishing tasks?" This has probably been one of the most frequently conducted experiments and yet the results seem to be related to the type of task selected for the study. In any case, I think it is a nonissue for practitioners as the question isn't, "Is this a task for an individual or for a group?" but, "How can I motivate anyone to do this task and help them gain satisfaction in the process?" The earliest studies were done by educators trying to determine if homework was done best individually or in groups. These days, with the competition from other areas for students' time and an awareness that some people work better together and some alone, we want to use whatever approach will motivate them to do any homework, and that there might have been a better way under laboratory conditions has little relation to our goal.

As leaders become aware of the concepts and applications described in this and similar publications and see how it can help them achieve their goals with groups they ask, "But if I use my understanding of group dynamics aren't I manipulating the group?" All leadership acts or interventions are manipulations in that they are attempts to move the group in some direction related to task accomplishment or group maintenance. Being aware of what is going on in a group and what the likely outcomes of various acts might be increases their influence. Manipulation is defined as "skillful or dexterous management"—an appropriate goal for group leaders. The greater concern is likely whether or not the acts are being used in a deceptive way against the best interests of others. Straightforward interventions by a leader are unlikely to be influential if they are against the best interests of the group as the group is stronger than the leader. And, leaders are unable to get a group to accept their goals until they have gained high-prestige status by accepting and working toward the goals of the group. Only coercion makes it possible to move a group toward ends that are not accepted.

SOCIAL CONTROL
AND INDIVIDUAL DEVELOPMENT

Many of the goals of human service workers are related to helping people learn, grow, and become more fully functioning as individuals. Providing information that will change behavior, teach new skills, or try to reverse self-defeating attitudes occupies much time and effort. The concepts outlined in this section indicate that much of an individual's behavior is tied up with the norms of the groups to which that person belongs. The new approach that has been consistently developing alongside these insights is that individual behavior can be influenced most effectively by working through the norms and standards of the groups to which the individuals belong. As the group with its norms and standards has become the target for change in the human services educational, treatment, and retraining programs, working with individuals in isolation from their reference groups has been on the wane.

Some of the changes are identified in the following examples:

Health Care. Home care treatment programs, where patients are worked with in their usual environment, are increasing. More attention is paid to preventive work through community groups, including many involved in health-care planning.

Training. There is a shift from attending workshops as individuals to on-the-job training with intact work groups, such as quality circles and team planning groups.

Counseling and Therapy. There is more use of family therapy approaches where the child, spouse, or parent seeking help is worked with in the context of the family, which becomes the focus for change.

Youth Work. Pioneers of group techniques are using more programs in natural locations, calling it street work, detached work youth, etc.

Recreation. Parents are involved with children in various programs, family camping, and child care (moving in more family life education programs). In using swimming as a vehicle for helping very young handicapped children, mothers are educated to believe that the child won't learn to swim until the mother is ready (until the family norms accept it, the child won't do it).

Education. Social control concepts are used in setting up learning groups, open classrooms, and teaching teams and, to some extent, in homogeneous grouping programs and students teaching students activities. The concepts are also in use in some programs designed to reduce school vandalism.

Institutional Change. The new field of organization development works from the foundation that changing norms and culture changes organizations.

Chapter 3

Understanding
Individuals in Groups

Understanding group behavior is advanced by having some knowledge of the importance of groups in social development and an awareness of the personality characteristics individuals bring with them to groups. Almost all of the emotional and social needs of individuals find their satisfaction in relationships with others. Individuals moving into a new group experience bring the influence of previous group experiences and typical modes of behavior are recognized. Many phenomena in groups are products of the members interacting and are unique to that situation. They cannot be explained by just looking at the behavior of individual members, for a group is more than the sum of its parts. Professional staffs with their background in psychology and guidance can recognize and appreciate much of the behavior they find in a group. Experience helps them to gain further understanding and enables them to make some hunches about the reason for individual behavior. But, they must be careful not to judge, and should assess motives in only a most cautious way. They have a serious responsibility to help the workers they supervise who have less training to recognize their limitations in doing any behavior analysis or in playing armchair psychologist.

EMOTIONAL NEEDS

Emotional needs have been categorized in different ways but usually include love, affection, security, recognition, a sense of belonging, and a feeling of self-worth. All of these needs find their fulfillment in relations with other people and there can be no affection or recognition without these other people. During a child's early years it is the family who provides most of the need satisfaction, but as a child grows older, friends at school and at home become increasingly important in satisfying needs. As mentioned earlier, the attraction of teen-agers to age-mate groups—because of their potential to satisfy these needs—may exceed attraction to family.

All behavior has some purpose or goal—people don't just "do things." If everything people do has some objective—some payoff—it helps to look for the payoff in trying to understand members' behavior. Motivation for behavior may be seen as partly unconscious with roots in early childhood. People may not know why they are doing certain things and perhaps ask others, "Why did I do that?" Yet the focus for group practitioners is not so much on trying to understand why participants do certain things but recognizing what they are getting out of their behavior, what needs are being satisfied. Regulating increases and decreases in need satisfaction may then influence behavior.

BEHAVIOR PATTERNS

Personality and behavior patterns are developed from inherited potentialities and life experiences. The goal of these behavior patterns is to provide physical security and satisfy physiological and emotional needs. As children are growing up, they find certain ways of finding satisfaction more successful than others. The behavior that is most successful tends to be continued and over a period of time develops into a usual way of doing things.

These usual ways of doing things or behavior patterns tend to develop fairly early in life and remain fairly stable thereafter. It is important that these behavior patterns remain fairly stable as they provide continuity and equilibrium. Consequently, healthy individuals have a built-in resistance to making major changes in these patterns. People have a great potential for learning and personal growth, especially within the parameters of their behavior patterns. Major changes in these basic patterns take place very slowly and usually with considerable effort.

GROWTH AND DEVELOPMENT

A useful framework for observing, understanding, and talking to others about individuals and groups is built around Schutz's three interpersonal relations orientations of *inclusion*, *control*, and *intimacy*. (See Part 2 for group applications and details.) All people are seen as having these three basic needs which start developing in early childhood with inclusion as the first need to achieve. The achievement of the developmental need in the second stage of growth (control) is partly dependent on the successful accomplishment of the previous need. While a certain level of inclusion and control behavior is developed in the first two years, there are further developments throughout life, but a child who has not developed behavior skills to meet these needs in early childhood is handicapped in further development throughout life.

Inclusion. Inclusion can be described as the need to establish and maintain satisfactory relations with other people. This is a need for belonging, to be wanted by other people, and, in turn, to be interested in them. The first year is a crucial time for the development of this sense of inclusion or belonging—of being wanted by one's parents and responding to their attention and care. Between four and six months of age, a hungry baby will grow quiet and show signs of pleasure when he hears someone coming, in anticipation of being cuddled and fed. A close physical relationship is assurance of being wanted. Children who have been deprived of an opportunity to develop a sense of inclusion such as may happen in a hospital or series of foster homes where no permanent mother figure is present, often develop shallow personalities typified by apathetic and listless behavior.

Control. Control is described as the need to establish and maintain a satisfactory relationship with people with respect to power and control. In the next developmental phase, children try to learn how they are able to influence and control some of the things that happen to them. They assert themselves showing that they are individuals with a mind of their own. This behavior is typical of the "terrible twos" who go around "feeling their oats." In this phase children need to learn that they are independent human beings who are able to control much of their lives, yet who are dependent on others for many things and are able to use the help and guidance of others in important matters. Through many types of negative behavior such as temper tantrums, resistance to toilet training, and frequent use of the word "no," they experiment with this control dimension to see how much influence they can have over parents and environment. As they learn to give and take, they work through the extreme alternatives of being compliant or rebellious—developing *interdependence* rather than dependence or independence. At this stage children need an opportunity to make decisions on their own, yet have guidance in doing it. Parental control that is too rigid or dominating robs them of the opportunity to make decisions or control and limits their development in this important area.

Intimacy. Intimacy is the need to establish and maintain a satisfactory relationship with people with respect to love and affection—the expressing of personal feelings. After children have developed a sense of belonging or inclusion and worked through their control of the environment, they start to develop an ability to establish close personal relations based on the open sharing of authentic feelings with parents and friends. Friendships take on a new meaning as a verbal interchange of feelings and reactions takes place. Developing intimacy is much like the problem of two cold porcupines who want to get close enough to share each other's heat but not so close as to get pricked by the quills.

As I have mentioned, the further development of these areas continues throughout life. An adolescent boy, for example, may be working on these concerns in ways which are quickly recognized. He tries to solve his needs for inclusion by joining several groups. Membership in these groups is most important to him and he will dress and talk differently, participate in activities which hold little interest for him, and resist the opposition of his parents in order to maintain his membership. Going steady in the early teens can also be an attempt to assure inclusion.

In the control area, the teenager is typically trying to establish a sense of identity—who he is and where he fits into things. He is concerned about what influence he has over things and that this influence on the shape of things is so minute. In daily activities, there is a lot of attention to the rules of games and sports. Sometimes it is more important to try and work out the rules and their application (was he safe or out?) than it is to continue playing the game. Control problems arise frequently in the home and at school, and the rebellious teenager is an example of inadequate solutions to control concerns.

Intimacy concerns develop in the teens as the expression of love and affection to parents is experimented with—am I too big to kiss? To cry? To lose my temper? Later, through the open sharing of hopes and fears higher levels of intimacy are explored. Finally, the relation between physical attraction and real affection or love becomes of paramount importance for many teenagers. It is common for adolescents to have difficulty expressing their true feelings about life or having reservations about being open in their relations with others and this often carries over into adulthood.

INTERPERSONAL BEHAVIOR IN ADULTS

All adults must work out reasonably satisfactory interpersonal relations in the areas of inclusion, control, and intimacy if they are to be happy and functioning fully, using all of their abilities. Now, while all people really desire to be included by others, some have had poor social experiences where they have been snubbed or hurt. Consequently, they may react by withdrawing on the basis that if I don't try to belong, I can't get hurt by being rejected. Or, they overcompensate and attempt to join numerous groups on the assumption that if I try to join lots of groups, some of them will be sure to accept me. Common concerns in the inclusion areas are that I am not interested in other people; that other people aren't interested in me.

In the control area, if people respect others and learn the give and take of interdependent behavior, they tend to be able to share control with others. If they have not learned this give and take or feel insecure with others, they may attempt to dominate all situations through autocratic behavior in order that what they desire will take place. Through this rigid control of situations individuals are able to minimize the risk of having to do things which other people may desire. It is a way of maintaining the safe, known situation and preventing having to do anything new that might show them up or upset them. The other way to resist control is to insist on individual rights and everyone doing his or her own thing. Then without any give and take a person won't get in a position to be controlled by others.

The ideal relationships in the intimacy area are close, open, authentic relations with others based on a feeling that other people like me and that I like other people. As I have mentioned, intimacy is similar to the problem of the frigid porcupines and people who have been hurt by getting too close may resist situations where feelings may be shared. They are underpersonal, neither seeking nor accepting close relations and are nervous about expressing how they really feel about things. As people move toward more open communication with others and can express both positive and negative feelings they are able to be more spontaneous in their actions and creative in their thinking.

All people cope with their problems in these areas by a variety of procedures and defenses which are perfectly normal. As we learn more about ourselves in relation to others and understand better why we do some of the things we do, we should be able to function more adequately in work and family situations. Self-insight also leads to improved social sensitivity which enables us to understand others better and help them achieve more productive and satisfactory relationships. This is one of the major qualities of the successful manager or supervisor.

WHAT INDIVIDUALS BRING
TO GROUP EXPERIENCES

People starting a new group experience bring with them the results of all previous relations with people and usual ways of dealing with needs for inclusion, control, and intimacy. These patterns show up in the attitudes, interests, and behavior of the new members. In observing member behavior and trying to understand it, some guidelines for valuable areas to consider may be helpful.

Similarities to Other Groups

New members coming into a group may find things that remind them of previous experiences, especially the people. Other members may remind them of youth with whom they went to school, or workmates from their jobs. The attitudes and feelings they had toward the former person may carry over and shape relations to the new group. This process is often called *transference*, suggesting that people often transfer feelings from one situation or relationship to another. Members are usually partially aware of these resemblances but can be helped to put them into the here and now by going around the group and saying (or thinking) who each person reminds them of.

Especially important are the transference reactions to the person in authority (teacher, staff worker, manager, or chairperson) as people usually have had very significant reactions to authority figures. And, group leaders should be aware that they are the target of both positive and negative feelings from the members through no fault of their own. Some members may also be ambivalent toward the leader and express positive and negative feelings in turn. The important thing is for authority figures to recognize these reactions, know that they may not have anything to do with them personally, and begin to work out a plan for dealing with them. These similarity reactions explain what many workers find dismaying in taking on a new group where some members accept them immediately and others reject them.

Members will, in all likelihood, have certain expectations for the worker, also based on previous experiences. If the worker or other members do not live up to these preconceived expectations there may be disappointment or anger coupled with aggressive behavior. The disappointed individual may react by trying to force the worker or other member into the expected pattern. Thus, workers who attempt to play a guiding, facilitating role with a new group may find themselves under great pressure to conform to expectations and tell the group what to do.

Usual Adjustment Techniques

Individuals moving into a group situation become anxious about their inclusion in the group and may feel threatened by the leader or other members. Their response to anxiety will be with a reaction designed to overcome, avoid, or circumvent the threatening situation in order to maintain their equilibrium and comfort. Most defensive reactions can be summarized as either moving toward (fight) or away from (flight) the source of anxiety. A member concerned about inclusion in the group could respond with *fight* by moving into an active role in the group and perhaps competing with the established leader. *Flight*, or moving away from, could be in the form of withdrawal and underparticipation, or using the old "foot out the door" approach, saying, "I'm not sure I can be in this group but am trying it out for a couple of sessions." Again, this approach of dealing with the problem (threat) rather than the symptom (shyness or aggression) will be most useful in developing a fully functioning group.

Hidden Influences and Agendas

Most people are members of several groups at the same time—family, church, work, and recreation. These groups all have their norms and standards and develop expectations with their members about how they are to behave. It is usual, then, that the members of the groups we are leading will be responding to pressures and expectations from these other groups when they are in our group. And, if the expectations conflict, a member may be under great pressure to decide which group's expectations to try to meet.

Another similar concept assumes that there are two levels of agendas or goals in a group including ones that are on the surface and ones that are hidden. A man who arrives late for a meeting may explain he missed his bus (surface agenda), but in reality wanted to miss dues collection because he was broke (hidden agenda). A college fraternity member may suggest putting on a play to raise money for the graduation dance while in reality he has just written a play as an English assignment (and got an "A" on it) and wants the group to put on his play. A group can be working on either agenda or both at the same time. Hidden agendas come to the surface as they are legitimized and encouraged by a climate of trust and acceptance, and groups that were working furiously and getting nowhere start moving ahead.

Testing the Authority Figure

It is important for members to have some sense of the group's status hierarchy for it to function smoothly without a lot of jostling for position, and the most important person to place is the assigned worker or supervisor. Consequently, whoever is seen as the authority figure receives a considerable amount of attention and scrutiny. Members want to get to know these potentially powerful people and figure out how they will handle different situations, when they step in and clamp down on the group, and what behavior they will reward and punish. Members must figure these things out before they can settle down and know who's going to do what to whom. The result is a great deal of behavior and interaction designed to test out the worker.

Children approach this testing phase rather openly, often directly asking the worker what he or she will do if they do such and such. If they are in doubt about the reality of the answer (if they feel, for instance, that it is a bluff) or it is not clear to them they will go ahead with the act in question to see what happens. Older youth and adolescents tackle the problem a little less directly, often pushing the worker into a corner little by little to see at what point he or she stops them. A cabin group during the first few nights of camp may talk louder and louder after lights out to see when the counselor will do what. Group members often horse around with one eye on each other and the other eye on the advisor to note his or her reaction.

Older youth and adults handle the testing more subtly by asking the worker how many other groups he or she has worked with and what happened in them. They ask questions or lead the discussion in such a direction as to find the age, marital status, education, economic and social position of the leader. They also try to determine why it is this person is working with their group, and on what basis he or she was selected.

Experienced workers plan ahead for this testing phase in a group, being ready to show some give-and-take yet establish the group structure and role they want rather clearly. They are also aware that the more "up front" and visible they are about who they are, their attitudes and expectations, the less will be the need for members to initiate this testing behavior. And, if their role does call for a "laid-back," observer-type style, they will expect a lot of testing behavior to be directed to them and not take it personally.

Chapter 4

Influencing Groups and Participants

The thesis presented in the previous two sections of this booklet suggests that groups are best thought of and worked with as social systems which have structures, norms, and usual ways of doing things. This section looks at influencing groups and participants and continues to develop this thesis by assuming that change is most easily accomplished by changing the social system, its norms, and the way it operates. We have looked at how group structures and norms develop, the purposes they serve for the group and individual members; let's now look at how they can be influenced to change in ways that will increase the effectiveness of the group and the self-actualization of the members.

New groups establish standards fairly quickly as they move to stabilize their membership and provide structures and expectations about their product. Once they are established, and found to be useful to the group and its members, they become regularized and are remarkably resistant to change. The standards of the group have been described as property of the group as a whole and are not greatly changed by shifts in group membership. New members influence very minor shifts in norms and it takes several generations of new members for this shift to become significant unless a "critical mass" of members change over, including most of the previous power structure.

INFLUENCING GROUPS

Group participation is the solvent to unstick the glue of standards. In my study of thirty-one educational/training programs, I concluded that growth was facilitated by being actively involved in the planning and decision-making process. Participation in planning maximizes initiative and responsibility among members and becomes a powerful motivator to follow up on groups' agreed-on plans even though they may "rock the boat" on the groups' previous standards. My studies and those of a number of others have demonstrated that group participation in planning, encouraging the involvement of all members, is a very effective method of changing group standards. If the entire group makes a decision about a change in standards and member behavior, it will likely happen. When a group "takes the pledge" together, such as in weight-watching groups, it is more powerful than when individuals make resolutions for change on their own.

Group standards are formed through member interaction and are owned by the total group and can be changed in the same way. Group planning and decision making facilitate the renewed interaction around these standards and are the most effective approaches to influencing change. Once a group starts to review its standards and consider setting new ones, the power of any changes will be increased if the group is functioning well and has good solidarity.

Bavelas (Cartwright & Zander, 1968, and Hare, 1976) demonstrated a group planning and decision-making model where he met with a group of women workers on a sewing operation and asked them if they would like to set a production goal for themsevles. After some discussion it was unanimously agreed to set a goal ten units higher than what they had been producing. Within five days this goal was exceeded and when the workers met to reconsider it, they set a new, permanent goal that was even higher. After six months they were still producing at that level. Some years later he used the same approach with a group of workers to change group standards and reduce assembly line blockages.

Similar studies have been made in hospitals where mothers having their first babies were instructed in good nutrition practices. Instituting a group discussion and decision-making approach doubled the number of women using the practices over the previous instructional methods of trying to influence behavior. Other studies have used the group participation method to pave the way for changing job assignments, introducing new work methods, and assigning some members to a new building.

In the early 1980s the group planning and decision-making model was seen in a very new light as it was the basis of the quality work circle associated with the very successful Japanese management style.[11] Quality work life programs in schools, agencies, and business have also made consistent

---

[11]William Ouchi, *Theory Z.* Reading, MA: Addison-Wesley, 1981.

use of the planning and decision-making model to achieve the participation, involvement, and group consensus needed to change group norms. A seven-year study of mine on influencing change in community service organizations also incorporated this model under the heading of Systems Improvement Research.[12] Such studies have increased our understanding of how best to use the participation model to influence groups.

INFLUENCING INDIVIDUALS

The attitudes and behavior of individuals, especially when they are in a group setting, are influenced by the standards of that group and the other groups to which that individual belongs. Individuals who misbehave in a classroom or youth group can be dealt with directly by the staff person, or an attempt can be made to tighten up the group's standards; this pressure on deviants to conform may reduce the unwanted behavior.

Previous discussions have presented ways to strengthen groups, facilitate the group's social control, and influence group standards. Other methods of influencing individuals include the following:

Form Groups. The planning and group decision-making model is sufficiently powerful in influence that it works by taking individuals who have no particular relationship with one another, putting them into groups, and encouraging them to consider new attitudes or behaviors. Individuals are more likely to carry out a new approach to something if they are supported in that action by others. Protest groups, affirmative action programs, religious cults, and youth retraining programs use this approach.

Modeling. Observing and identifying with the behavior of others are important influences on many people. Research has shown that youth typically model some of the behavior of their adult leaders and that the quality of the leader's attitudes and behavior was directly related to the development of the youth in similar areas. A camp study showed that youth who

---

[12]Hedley G. Dimock, "A Study of Systems Improvement Research in the administration, service delivery and policy planning of four community serving organizations." Guelph, Ontario: University School of Continuing Education, University of Guelph, 1981.

were well accepted by other campers had behavior that was very "contagious." Efforts by adults to increase their attractiveness to other members typically expand their influence (Zander, 1982).

Peer Training. Social support for new behavior is generated by peers taking responsibility for training each other in the new behaviors rather than bringing in an expert or outsider. Peer training is especially powerful in schools, universities, disadvantaged groups, ethnic groups, and other groups that may have uniqueness that distances them from "outsiders." When combined with using a desirable role model in the form of the peer trainer/coach a double influence is produced. This understanding has led to self-help groups, networking systems, and community-based personal development groups.

Providing Information and Utilization Frameworks. Another important tool for shaping behavior is helping participants develop insights about an experience so they can generalize and apply the learning to another situation. These generalizations provide a utilization framework for experiences. The frequent use of immediate rewards develops conditioning—a specific response to that situation. Only when the response can be understood and applied on a problem-solving basis to another situation can it be considered learning. For example, when children discover that touching a familiar pot-bellied stove produces burns, they may keep away from it because of the conditioning process of touching and getting burned. Only when they develop an understanding that a variety of receptacles that contain burning materials are also hot and will burn, have they really learned about hot stoves. It is essential to the growth process that an individual be able to predict the consequences of a variety of possible behaviors in a situation. These predictions are based on insights gleaned through previous experiences and tested against the utilization framework that person has developed. Consequently, new information to be maximally influential must fit into the already-established utilization framework of members to help to modify the frameworks by showing relationships among experiences that will enable participants to more accurately predict the results of future actions.

Experiential Learning. People learn according to what they experience in trying to satisfy their various needs. Proving influential information has impact when it fits into utilization frameworks—a person's usual way of looking at things—or by developing insights and connections about behavior and outcomes, modifies the framework. Experiences that are "learning by doing" oriented are particularly influential in modifying attitudes and behavior by using both thinking and feeling processes. A group climate of high acceptance facilitates members trying out new behavior in a "learning by doing" orientation. Immediate feedback saying how a particular behavior affected the other members, helps a person judge the appropriateness of the action. The clearer and more specific the feedback, and the more closely it follows the action described, the more influential will be the information.

Dealing with the "here and now" as contrasted with the "then and there" is often used to differentiate experiential learning from other approaches. Thus, trying to improve the way members handle conflict may include presenting a new approach, seeing a film of individuals using the approach, and reading about its effectiveness in other situations. To have experiential learning, the members must try it out in real situations and get feedback on their attempts to implement it. If the members do find the approach useful and start to reorganize their utilization frameworks to include it, then getting a lot of support and reinforcement for the new behavior will help them follow through with the change. The greatest resistance to influence attempts occurs at the point the individual has tried it out and is considering incorporating it for keeps.

POWER AND INFLUENCE

Nothing succeeds like having the winning hand. Power and influence are the winning hand—the name of the game. As we have seen there are two ways to get power and influence in a group. One is through the formal or external system that assigns a position and power to give certain rewards or punishments. Rewards may include hiring staff or selecting volunteers, job assignments, office and equipment allocations, disbursement of funds, media contacts, promotion, selecting the group members for special activities (playing on an all-star team or attending the mayor's luncheon), or whatever the currency of rewards are in that system.

The other way people may gain power is by increasing their attractiveness to others. This is called prestige power and may be gained by being an attractive person (good grooming, well dressed, articulate speaker), doing favors for others, or giving recognition, approval, and a lot of personal attention. Some people see the influence process like a banking activity— how much they owe others versus how much they are owed—and are reluctant to use their influence for fear of depleting their account. Studies have shown that as most people gain influence through personal prestige they do use it, and this further enhances their prestige providing they don't go too far and do something that ignores the group's standards.

IN A NUTSHELL

People who meet in groups tend to form standards of operation and behavior in order to operate more effectively as a group and maintain themselves as a group. Members are expected to conform to these norms. In this process of social control a group derives its power to control deviant members from its solidarity. The more cohesive the group, the more it is able to control its members. Members of cohesive groups who find the group putting pressure on them to abide by group standards may either modify their behavior or leave the group, depending on their reasons for membership and the attractiveness of the group to them.

While almost all members contribute leadership to the group at one time or another, groups develop a leadership hierarchy and award status in relation to position. This personal status is gained by helping the group be successful and gives the owner considerable influence. Leadership functions either help the group to accomplish its goals or to maintain itself as a group. The most effective mix of task and group-building functions depends on a number of situational variables, and diagnosing these variables increases group influence.

A group is a social system with structure, norms, and usual ways of doing things. Deliberately planned actions to strengthen or modify that system are a powerful approach to enhancing learning and personal growth, group productivity, and organizational revitalization and change.

REFERENCES AND BIBLIOGRAPHY

Cartwright, Dorwin and Alvin Zander (editors). *Group Dynamics* (3rd Edition). New York: Harper and Row, 1968.

Dimock, Hedley G. *Intervention and Collaborative Change*. Guelph, Ont.: University of Guelph, 1981.

Dimock, Hedley G. *The Selection and Training of Community Recreation Leaders*. Montreal: Sir George Williams Centre for Human Relations and Community Studies, Concordia University, 1979.

Fiedler, Fred. *Theory of Leadership Effectiveness*. New York: McGraw-Hill, 1967.

Fiedler, Fred and Martin Chemers. *Leadership and Effective Management*. Glenview, IL: Scott, Foresman, 1974.

Hare, A. Paul. *Handbook of Small Group Research* (2nd Edition). New York: Free Press, 1976.

Hersey, Paul and Ken Blanchard. *Management of Organizational Behavior* (3rd Edition). New York: Prentice-Hall, 1977.

Napier, Rodney and Matti Gershenfeld. *Groups: Theory and Experience* (2nd Edition). Boston: Houghton Mifflin, 1981.

Shaw, Marvin E. *Group Dynamics* (2nd Edition). New York: McGraw-Hill, 1981.

Sherif, Muzafer and Carolyn Sherif. *Social Psychology.* New York: Harper and Row, 1969.

Stogdill, Ralph M. *Handbook of Leadership.* New York: Free Press, 1974.

Zander, Alvin. *Making Groups Effective.* San Francisco: Jossey-Bass, 1982.

Part 2:
How to Observe Your Group

Chapter 5

Ways of Looking
at Group Development

A framework or theory of how groups grow and develop is needed to determine areas for observation and data collection. A framework around which to view a group's development is necessary to understand groups, make predictions about groups, communicate with others about groups, and help groups become more effective. There are many and varied ways of looking at the growth of a group. The range is from seeing groups as miniature civilizations that grow in relation to the challenges present and decline when they become inflexible and rest on their past accomplishments, to finding typical patterns in the frequency and focus of interactions within the group. Several group development theories are presented here to illustrate some of the most widely accepted viewpoints and to provide a sound basis from which can be selected the concepts that make most sense to the reader. And, all of these viewpoints have been used extensively by the author in helping human service workers (recreation, social work, education, and health services) understand what typically happens in their groups.

VIEWPOINT 1—DEVELOPMENTAL AREAS

The two major contributions of a framework of group development are to identify the areas that are worth observing in a group and to help explain the relationship among various happenings in the group. The areas of group development identified in this viewpoint are the ones I have used most extensively in my thirty years of working in community agencies, classrooms, training groups, and organizational consultations. They have been regularly updated and most recently were revised to diagnose organizational well-being. The five areas presented in this viewpoint—climate, involvement, interaction, cohesion, and productivity—provide a crisp, yet comprehensive overview of any group. And, while the five dimensions do not constitute

59

an integrated theory of group development, they can be easily used with the other theories presented here. It has been found that by observing, understanding, and giving attention to these five areas, groups can improve their procedures, accomplish higher-level tasks, and enable members to satisfy more of their own needs and interests.

Group Climate

Group climate includes both the physical climate or set-up and the emotional climate which can be equally important to the well-being and growth of the group. The physical surroundings should encourage the work of the group—its task accomplishment and morale of the members. Seating arrangements, lighting, ventilation, proximity of members, and pleasantness of the surroundings can all affect the group. A gym floor is a poor location for a small-group planning session, a theatre-style classroom is a poor place for a teachers' meeting, and rows of benches in a club room do not lend themselves to a board meeting. Moving outdoors to a shady area of grass makes for pleasant surroundings but reduces attention span and interaction possibilities. Tables and chairs increase the orderly decision-making activities of a group, yet an open circle of chairs may result in more personal communication and expression of feeling. Nonverbal communication is quite important in some groups and if all the members can't see one another such a group would be handicapped much the same as a group where members couldn't all hear one another.

Perhaps even more important is the emotional climate of the group which determines the security and acceptance of members. A friendly, informal, accepting climate can encourage trust among members and by decreasing anxiety, help members to be themselves and use their resources. Expectations for the group by the organization (rules and regulations) and the style of the leader can also influence group climate.

Group Involvement

Involvement refers to the extent members are occupied or absorbed with the group. Involvement is usually determined by attraction to the other members in the group and to the activities or product of the group. Involvement may also be encouraged through the overall status or prestige the group has in the community. Having some stake in the outcome of the group's work also increases involvement.

The key questions in assessing involvement are: why are the members here, what attracts them to the group, and what personal needs are they meeting by belonging? Levels of involvement show up in lateness, absenteeism and turnover, and in attention and commitment to group tasks. Thus, the levels of participation and involvement are closely related. Groups with high involvement are most likely to develop a sense of solidarity and cohesion, and become strong, healthy groups.

Involvement can be encouraged by increasing the attractiveness of the group's activities, the satisfaction members receive from interacting with the other members, and the prestige gained through the group's accomplishments. Opportunities for members to participate in setting their own work goals and procedures are usually very successful in increasing involvement. The use of intergroup competition, awards, and prizes often increases involvement in the short term, yet if they don't relate to the real needs and interests of the members, they will quickly wear out.

Group Interaction

Interaction is a key dimension in group development, for the more members interact with one another, the more likely the group will develop and accomplish its tasks. Groups with high rates of interaction tend to be healthier and more productive than groups where there is low interaction or just interaction among subgroups. Generally, the more people interact with each other, the more likely they are to be attracted to each other and develop solid relationships. Interaction can be encouraged by arranging the physical set-up so people can see and talk easily to each other, and selecting activities that facilitate members interacting and working together. Group decision-making activities, card playing, or going caroling as a service project promote more interaction than playing water polo, having running races, or listening to a speech.

Emotional climate is closely related to interaction. Members who feel secure and accepted in a group setting are encouraged to interact with others and express some of their real feelings, problems, and concerns. Relationship problems, subgrouping, conflict, and the status hierarchy may get in the way of free interaction. An analysis of the roles of group members described as Viewpoint II gives a great deal of information about the interaction of a group.

Group Cohesion

Cohesion, the fourth major dimension of group growth, is often called solidarity or unity. It relates to the strengths of the relationships among the members, and can be assessed by determining how well members know and understand each other, and by the degree of feeling they have of the group as theirs. In many ways, cohesion is a product of climate, involvement, and interaction, but there are groups where cohesion is high, but interaction may not be well distributed or the emotional climate may create insecurity.

Groups with a high degree of solidarity or cohesion are most able to encourage deviant members to accept or compromise with group standards through the group pressure they can exert. Behavior and attitudes are most likely to be influenced in rather highly cohesive groups that are attractive to the individual members.

A growing group generally becomes more cohesive although occasionally a group can become too cohesive for its own good, as when members refuse to admit any newcomers. At this stage of standing pat and keeping the same membership, the group may not continue to grow and mature.

A cohesive group pulls together toward common objectives. It is this solidarity that helps the group to maintain itself as a group and provides the pressure to encourage members to conform to group standards and work toward common goals.

Group Productivity

The productivity and accomplishments of a group provide much of the motivation for membership and are usually the focus for group interaction. All groups are seen by their members as having goals or tasks to accomplish and the movement toward these goals influences the satisfaction of the members and the pride in the group as a whole. It is important to study the origin of a group's goals; the integration of individual goals into group goals; the plans or procedures, if any, designed to facilitate the accomplishment of these goals; and the ability of the group to follow the plans and achieve the goals. This involves areas of goal setting, decision making, and implementation.

Styles of leadership within the group and the distribution of member roles play an important part in productivity. As suggested in Part 1, the appropriateness of leadership style in relation to the situational factors of the group was a major influence on group morale and productivity. Hence, all identified roles in the group—chairperson, advisor, coach, recorder, supervisor, or instructor—should be examined closely to note their impact on the group and its effectiveness.

This approach to group development suggests that there are five major group dimensions which are closely related to one another and together account for most of the dynamics in any group. As these areas are assessed, analyzed, and understood, and facilitative plans worked out in a systematic fashion, a group can be helped to grow, increasing the satisfaction of members and the task accomplishments of the group. A Group Observation Guide is presented in Chapter 6 that lays out the major points to be assessed under these five headings.

VIEWPOINT II—MEMBER ROLES

Leadership may be defined in functional terms as acts which help the group to accomplish its goals or maintain itself as a group. All interactions within a group may be classified as helping the group to accomplish its task, helping the group to maintain itself as a group, or not serving any group function.

The member roles viewpoint of group development implies that a group needs both task and group-building-oriented participation of members if it is to grow and become fully productive. All participation can be recorded and classified as one or another of the fifteen functions or roles. The Group Observation Guide in Chapter 6 has fourteen areas in which to classify the interaction acts of the members. The division is as follows:

Task Roles

1. Defines problems
2. Seeks information
3. Gives information
4. Seeks opinions
5. Gives opinions
6. Tests feasibility

Group-Building and Maintenance Roles

7. Coordinating
8. Mediating-harmonizing
9. Orienting-facilitating
10. Supporting-encouraging
11. Following

Individual Roles (nonfunctional)

12. Blocking
13. Out of field
14. Digressing

Not only does a group need both task and group-building functions, but it needs appropriate functions at the right time. When a football team isn't functioning well, an analysis is made of the different positions. The center may be snapping the ball a bit late or the guards may not be blocking their men. All of the roles need to function well if the team is to operate smoothly and win games. In a football squad a man is assigned to each position and he knows his job. But a group may have many roles or functions that are not played and the members may not be aware of these omissions. A review of the roles taken in the group compared to the roles that a group requires (such as the eleven given) points up the gaps. Filling the gap requires recognition of the importance of these roles or group positions and an ability of the members to take these roles when needed. The ability to take a wide variety of roles as they are needed in different situations is called role flexibility and is likely the most valuable attribute of a fully functioning group member.

The extent to which the eleven essential functions are taken becomes evident through group observation. The performance of these functions may be poorly spread around the group with only two or three people attempting to fill all the positions. This keeps other members from assuming responsibility and is unlikely to utilize the skills of all the members. Members may not have the opportunity to practice new roles and grow accordingly if two or three people dominate. And, if there is domination by a few, the resources of new members are not utilized.

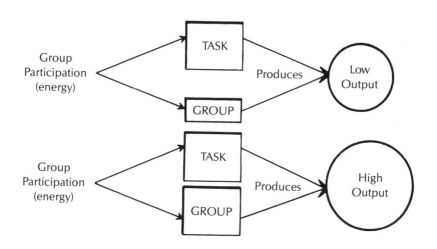

Giving major attention to task roles produces lower output (productivity) than giving attention to both task and group roles.

Role flexibility, inadequate role distribution, and missing group functions once identified through observation and analysis can be improved by discussion and agreement of group needs, and the practice of the needed roles in the group. Individual training through reality practice in out-of-group situations is also helpful.

Groups, during their initial stages of development, tend to be primarily task oriented. Almost all the participation is at a task level, such as giving opinions and giving information. The development of the group, as well as its productivity, is limited unless it can move into the group-building area.

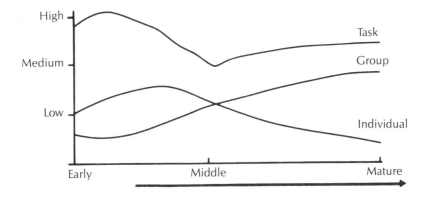

Mature groups show a reasonable balance of task and group roles. Individual roles increase in the early stages of development and drop off during the mature stage.

Figure 4

In fact, the development of a group can be charted by comparing the percentage of task roles to group-building and nonfunctional roles. The early stages are characterized by a high proportion of task roles with individual roles growing in number. As growth progresses, group roles rise and individual roles drop off.

In summary, then, a group has to acquire a balance of task and group functions if it is to utilize all its potential as a group. Typically, groups are task oriented and need help in learning group-building roles. Certain functions are required at specific times and these can often be determined through observation and analysis. It is also helpful if the roles are widely distributed among members and all assume responsibility for the functions the group requires.

The member function viewpoint of group development is of special interest to educational organizations because of the close relation between the flexibility of an individual's functions in groups and other social situations. The healthy, well-functioning person has been described as one who is able to be flexible in his social roles and behavior. An important part of personality development is learning to take a wide variety of social roles skillfully and realistically, developing a large repertoire of them, and becoming adroit in shifting from one role to another as the situation changes.

To be sure, the eleven task and group-building roles are but a few of the important social roles in life. Yet, the learning by an individual of the skills of shifting from one role to another and the ability to assess a situation to know what roles are useful is an important contribution to personal growth. Role flexibility coupled with the effective use of task and group-building roles is an indicator of a flexible, adaptive person who has little susceptibility to behavior disorders.

VIEWPOINT III—INTERPERSONAL RELATIONS

The following framework for observing, understanding, and talking to others about groups is a continuation of the one started in Part 1, describing the growth, development, and basic needs of individuals. It is based on three basic interpersonal relations needs proposed by Schutz (1958, 1966) and has been put into a developmental framework based on my experiences over a number of years and the contributions of a considerable number of writers about group development. The framework assumes that groups have three basic developmental needs, namely: inclusion, control, and intimacy or openness. As in individual growth, the development of a group is handicapped if each dimension is not resolved in its order of emergence. Thus, a group that has basic problems of membership (inclusion) and control is not likely to develop very far in the area of intimacy and openness. Figure 5 suggests how this works.

Figure 5 is not meant to imply that a group works on only one factor in growth at a time or always in order. Rather, it suggests a usual order of development, but once a group is underway, it moves from dimension to dimension as problems come up. In working on and managing these problems, the development of that factor is moved that much further ahead. Over a period of time, the same three issues of inclusion, control, and intimacy continue to surface but at higher or more sophisticated levels. For example, in the early life of a group it may be sufficient for members to ascertain the degree of membership they hold in the group. Later, they may want to experiment with reaching out to bring in a fringe member of the

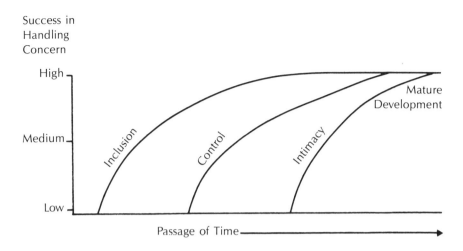

Each dimension moves forward one at a time and each requires the previous one
to be resolved before it can develop adequately.

Figure 5

group who has been a cautious participant. And later, they may want to
test the quality of their acceptance in the group as they take on more true-
to-life roles that are perhaps deviant from usual expectations for membership. Figure 6 attempts to picture this repetition of concerns as a helix whose
circles indicate work on each factor and, as the group develops, the work
is at a higher level of development.

Most groups start off dealing with these three factors in order and my
studies of project groups found that members characterized their early,
middle, and late phases with descriptions consistent with inclusion, control, and intimacy. While a middle stage of development may include issues
of inclusion and intimacy or openness, most groups describe the
predominating theme as one of control.

Schutz (1966) has done some research which suggests that groups formed
of members who are compatible on these three dimensions will be more
effective than other groups. Thus, if a group has some members who want
to be in control and others who are prepared to accept that control, it will
function better than a group with "all chiefs and no Indians." The idea of
creating balanced groups where members meet each other's needs sounds
good and is worth exploring further.

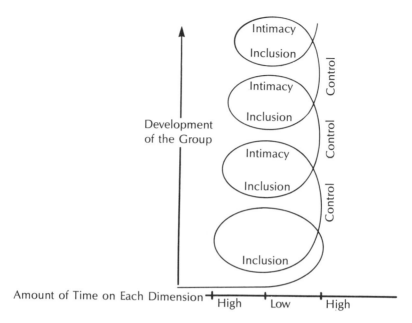

As the group grows, the three factors are dealt with again and again at a higher level of resolution and for a shorter space of time.

Figure 6

Typical Group Development

While it is always difficult and risky to generalize about the growth of a group without knowing its physical surroundings, members, or goals, the following description creates a framework within which your group can be looked at and compared to other groups. The forms of expression of typical group concerns and the relationships among them may stimulate your thinking about linkages that will make sense in understanding your group. And keep in mind that during all three phases there are the "words and the music"—what the group is talking about or apparently working on and what interpersonal concern the group may really be dealing with at that time.

Inclusion Stage

During the first few meetings of a new group the members try to get to know each other to see who they will like and who will accept them. They usually do this by talking about the weather, current events, or perhaps sharing some recent experience. This is an effort to establish their *inclusion* in the group and to be recognized and accepted as a member. Part of becoming a member is to know what the group expects of you so you can figure out whether you really want to belong. And, it helps for the other group members to know what you expect from the group. As members balance out what they will need to give to get accepted and what they can expect to get if they are accepted, they establish their commitment to the group. Some members find this process easiest if they jump into the group activities or discussions, while others find that sitting on the sidelines and watching works best for them. This creates over and under participators and often becomes an issue in the group. While the words are "participation," the music is "what are the acceptable gives and gets?" in the group.

Members may also ask about the goals of the group, the background of the organization to which the group belongs, or the qualifications of the person in a leadership position as a way of sorting out what is going to be expected of them. Some groups facilitate this process by having orientation sessions where participants are told what is expected of them. Some groups conduct an interest census, where participants describe the interests which they hope the group will work toward. Sometimes, too, there is a formal initiation and acceptance ceremony which establishes membership (churches, service clubs, fraternities, youth groups, and athletic teams).

As this phase moves toward closure, members are usually able to determine who are solidly in the group, who are halfway in, and who are the fringe members. Groups who are still unresolved about this concern may establish attendance requirements (anyone who misses two meetings in a row is out) or other artificial regulations to clarify the inclusion issue. At this time, too, members may resist taking on new members and treat outsiders coolly as ways of maintaining the comfort of the membership they have worked so hard to establish. All in all, this phase has been a time of hope and trepidation.

Control Stage

Members usually leave the inclusion stage with a pretty clear picture of the amount of acceptance or prestige given to each group member. In the control phase members are trying to figure out "who gets to do what to whom." This interest builds on the acceptance hierarchy established and turns it into a status or power hierarchy. I call it working out a "pecking order" (the order in which chickens feed) or "gate order" (the order in which cows pass through the pasture gate into the barn). As attention shifts to decision making and who is able to influence, the group members jockey for position in the status hierarchy. Members are interested in figuring out their influence potential and how much they are prepared to have the group control them. Typically, there is an increase in hostility and bickering over minor points as members attempt to consolidate their position in the group.

The group, to move through this stage, requires some agreement about how decisions will be made—majority vote, consensus, referral to executive committee, or whatever. Sometimes a member will try to take over the group (which makes it safe for that person) or try to prevent any decision-making procedures from being established (which is another way of keeping the group safe as no decisions can be made to require the person to do something undesired). Once the leadership hierarchy is established and procedures worked out for making decisions, members are able to relax a bit and start enjoying themselves. Any "gate order," even if you come in last, is better than none, as ambiguity about position and continuous conflict in pushing for position is very unsettling. Groups and organizations often try to facilitate this issue by assigning specific ranks or positions to members.

Groups that work through these control issues at an adequate level are able to share the leadership functions among all the members and are consequently able to utilize the full resources in the group. No single member becomes indispensable and all share in accepting responsibility. As the group increases its solidarity during this phase and sets challenging but attainable goals, it also develops standards for its members which help to facilitate the movement toward agreed-upon goals. As a result, the work level or productivity of the group increases.

With satisfactory solutions to the problems in the control area, there is a great sense of accomplishment in the group. This may create a very high happiness level where the group feels it is really great and attempts to maintain this group harmony past the point of usefulness. As far as the group is concerned, there is no project too great, no task too difficult for it to handle. The recognition that this attitude is unrealistic and there are other things to accomplish leads to the next stage of openness and member authenticity.

Intimacy Stage

The major concern during this stage of group development is working out how open or authentic members are prepared to be with one another considering the purposes of the group. The group starts giving less attention to the status hierarchy and the key players, and more attention to the ideas and unique abilities of each member. There is an acceptance of individual differences and less concern about deviants conforming to group standards as this stage is successfully resolved. The creative members of the group play an increasingly important role and leadership shifts among members in terms of the group task or situation at hand.

Members of the group feel secure with one another and as the trust level develops, there is more sharing of real feelings. This authentic communication and intimacy increases the attraction of the group for members. As personal feelings and opinions are communicated in a direct and open fashion, the data available for problem solving rapidly increases. Efficiency rises as no time is wasted trying to figure out what participants are really saying, or worrying about what strategy is being used on the group. Now each member can be known and treated as an individual, and the unique abilities of each member can be used for the betterment of the group. As the group is no longer hung up on power and control, it may give up "majority rule" and move to group consensus, where all members are committed to action and taking responsibility for implementation. Resolving conflict is no longer the concern it was during the control stage. With the new level of trust and openness, it can be used creatively for the good of the group.

Summary

Groups that have resolved the usual concerns of members in the areas of inclusion, control, and intimacy are solid, cohesive groups with members who know where they stand in relation to one another and to the task of the group. Leadership is typically shared in these mature groups and the team leader or supervisor is able to either delegate or assign responsibilities with a high level of member acceptance. While there are clear standards and expectations, the group, because of its solidarity and maturity, can tolerate conflict and a creative minority among its members. A well-developed group is a learning, growing experience for members, contributing to their self-actualization and physical and mental health.

Abortive groups usually get stuck trying to sort out the concerns in one of these developmental areas—usually control. After trying to manage key issues for a while, groups may pretend they have been worked out and that all is well. Whether it is a family or work group the facade is easily shattered and group growth, as well as member growth, is stunted.

Individuals who have had several successful group experiences and thus have high expectations for a new group, and professionals whose occupations suggest they should have mature groups, are likely candidates for an abortive group. These people are often unwilling to go through the trials and tribulations of building a healthy group and imagine they can establish trust and openness by group proclamation. It is like deciding to be an Olympic winner without going through the training.

Groups undergoing constant crisis or who are under continuous pressure or stress from the external environment are also likely to have their development stunted. During the economic recession of the 1980s many work groups that had it pretty well together regressed to immature levels of bickering, hostility, and distrust when their organizations started firing staff. It is common, too, that a usually successful sports team will scapegoat a member after experiencing tension from a string of losses.

Groups are usually rather predictable because of normative processes and self-sustaining goals. An awareness of usual developmental needs and dynamics helps members and group facilitators figure out what is happening in their group and intervene in ways that will encourage further group growth.

VIEWPOINT IV—WORK AND EMOTION

The work and emotion theory of group development started with the work of Bion at the Tavistock Institute in England (1961) and was given sequential stages for application by associates of the National Training Laboratories in Group Development in the United States (Stock & Thelen, 1958; Bennis, 1964). The theory has been used extensively in classroom groups, human relations training groups, industrial work groups, and community groups. In order to understand group phenomena, the activities of the group are analyzed in terms of the *level of work* (a little to a lot) and *emotional content*. The emotional content is assessed on the continuums of fight versus flight, pairing versus counterpairing, dependency versus counterdependency, or some combination of these three dimensions.

Flight. Avoidance or denial of the problem, issue, or task.

Fight. Hostility and assertion, a direct confrontation of the problem.

Pairing. Expression of intimacy, acceptance, and supportiveness.

Counterpairing. Rejecting warmth and supportiveness of others.

Dependency. Reliance on a person (leader, teacher, supervisor) or thing external to membership (policies, experts, regulations).

Counterdependency. Rejection or denial of authority or outside influences.

These categories may be used to describe the group as a whole, e.g., "the group is in a state of flight," or an individual, "Dale appears to be very dependent on the group worker."

Now the work and emotional components of group life are so interrelated that one never occurs without the other. Consequently, the group is always analyzed in terms of its level of work and primary emotional theme (or themes). The emotional quality often determines the level of work and vice versa. A group where members are concerned about their status and are directing *fight* to that concern, probably produces little work. Likewise, a group with an overwhelming task might handle it with emotional *flight*. At many times a group will not be openly verbalizing an emotional theme such as flight, but the activities of the group can be understood when it is assumed that they are attempting to avoid a problem or task. For example, a group may express interest in a task and apparently be working hard at it, but the more it works, the farther it gets from accomplishing that task. This behavior can be understood if it is viewed as *flight* and assumed that underneath the surface the group doesn't want to accomplish the task or is afraid to try to accomplish it for some reason. The observer must ask, "What is this group really trying to do? It is acting as if it resisted or rejected the worker; it is running from conflict of subgroups" and so forth.

Phases of Group Growth

Groups vary among the emotional themes they appear to be expressing and the level of work and its relationship to emotionality. When a group is reflective and orderly, and members are listening to one another, it is primarily in a work phase. In response to individual needs or stress it may be disorderly and hostile. At such a time, the group is seen as primarily in an emotional state.

The level of work can range from a low of being unrelated to the objectives and tasks of the group, to a high where there is active problem solving and creative, productive work. The work level of a group usually increases as it continues to meet and emotionality recedes. While there are no exact patterns for groups, the following phases can be expected.

Early Phase

The early phase is characterized by orientations toward authority and more generally, the distribution of power in the group. The usual stereotypes that prevail during this phase are that every group needs a strong, competent leader who can move the group toward its goals. It is also believed that certain "necessary" information should be forthcoming (job title, education, family), as each member sees other members as individuals and needs to establish their position in the hierarchy in relation to that member. This phase is characterized by concerns about authority and the usual reaction is one of dependence and flight.

If the structure of the group is seen as vague and unclear, and the leader seems weak and ambiguous, a search for goals and objectives—a common group task—results, yet the source of anxiety is the authority figure, not the group's goal. Weak authority figures facilitate the rise of a group member who is assertive and claims to have previous group experience. Dependence on this person works well momentarily, but is doomed to failure. During this phase most behavior is individually oriented and the work level is low.

Middle Phase

As the early phase closes there is considerable interaction with the worker or authority figure in an attempt to size the worker up and determine what rewards and punishments may be forthcoming from various behaviors. It is important to know how much power the worker will have so members will know how much power, and in which areas, is left for them to share. There is more *fight* behavior among members as they consolidate their positions in the group (this happens in the early phase of children's groups). If the worker is directive and encourages dependence, the power struggle among the members is less intense as there is less power up for grabs. But if the authority figure is permissive and unassertive, there will be a more intense power struggle and more counterdependent behavior toward the worker. It will take the form of resisting the authority of the worker, and playing down the value of opinions and suggestions of the worker. There may even be some discussion about the usefulness and competence of the worker, and perhaps suggestions of ways the group could work well on its own.

As the leadership hierarchy becomes more firmly established, there is a lot of pairing and subgrouping among members. Two subgroups may compete for power at this stage and surprisingly, neither may win as power often shifts to the neutral independent group. The *pairing* builds relationships and support which makes the group more relaxed and enjoyable. The close of this phase may see a honeymoon characterized by "sweetness and light" if the group feels it has worked through its conflicts and disagreements, and feels comfortable with the authority figure.

Mature Phase

The *pairing* and good feelings members develop during the middle phase increases the attractiveness and cohesion of the group. Group standards evolve and there is pressure on deviants to conform to these standards. The group becomes more able to maintain itself as a group and operate smoothly within the standards it has set for itself. While the work level during the middle phase varies, this phase sees a higher level of work and more satisfaction with the work among members.

The destructive conflict and hostility that developed during the middle phase may have been managed artificially with a tacit agreement of group harmony. And, like real honeymoons, this tends to cover over the expression of any differences or negative feelings. The primary challenge of this mature phase is for the group to work through the compromise and harmony veneer and free up openness and authenticity so it can use the full resources of its members. In recognizing the limitations of the group and the limitations of individual members, a group can build around them. Maturity is measured by how effectively the group manages tensions, conflicts, and the deviant or creative behavior of its members. Mature groups collect relevant data on individual and group performance and use it to revise their ways of working—trust, openness, and a readiness to deal with real issues are essential if this feedback is to be used successfully.

The mature phase is one of integration, group flexibility, open expression of individual feelings, and task accomplishment. It is generally characterized as high work and *pairing*, though the group's interdependence is also evident.

In summary, the most noteworthy contribution of this theory is its clarity about the importance of working through the roles and relations with the authority figure in the group. Groups that are unable to get at and deal with this person become stunted in their growth or disintegrate. Group workers taking their members through this tricky and unpleasant phase can gain security in understanding that the testing behavior and hostility has little to do with them personally. Workers whose leadership styles shift from directing to coaching and facilitating in pace with the growth of the group (see Part 1) will minimize the trauma of this experience. Effective leadership can also be seen as helping the group through these three phases that have been characterized as (1) *flight* and *dependence*, (2) *fight* and *counterdependence*, and (3) *pairing* (and interdependence).

VIEWPOINT V—TORI AND TRUST FORMATION

Jack Gibb's TORI theory of personal, group, and organizational development is based on trust—trust in one's self, in other people, and in the organizations and structures they can create. The framework of this theory is based on four dimensions and TORI is an acronym for these key factors: Trust, Openness, Realization, and Interdependence. But *trust* is the basic component on which the theory is built, for it is assumed that without a continuous increase in the trust level in a group, the other three factors will not be able to develop. Gibb sees fear, a symptom of unresolved trust, as the most crippling feature in personal and group development. People grow as they increase their trust and acceptance of themselves and others. Most nonfunctional behavior of individuals and groups can be understood as fear and the facades and defenses it creates. Group experiences where members learn how to create trusting, accepting climates encourage individual development and also healthy, productive groups.

In the TORI framework there are four dimensions or modal concerns in group growth. *Acceptance* is concerned with the achievement of membership in the group based on trust. *Data flow* is concerned with opening valid, spontaneous communication in the group and translating these data into decision making and choices. *Goal formation* has to do with determining member wants and integrating them into problem solving and group action planning, with a goal of productive, creative work. *Control* is concerned with leadership, power, and organizational structures that can be developed into freedom-giving, flexible forms. According to TORI theory, the most revealing aspect of a group's development is a description of the ways in which the early fears in the group are resolved by an increase in trust. The chart on TORI Group Development Process describes some of the common fears and problems of early group life and what they are replaced with as the group develops more trust in later phases.

TORI is essentially a developmental theory of group growth as there is an optimal sequence in the development of the four dimensions. Yet, the four factors are processed throughout the life of the group and continually flow together and build on each other. Certainly trust and acceptance compose the catalyst for the development of the other three factors if, in fact, they aren't the essential prerequisite. Trusting is an open process and any high-trust group can't help but be open to highly unpredictable and emergent outcomes. Clearly, this is the most humanistic theory I have presented and as one of its most important contributions is its openness and flexibility, it would be inappropriate for it to predetermine usual stages of group growth.

TORI Group Development

Modal Concern	Individual Behavior	Early Development	Later Development
Trust Acceptance	Accepting self and others	Conformity Fear of adequacy	Diversity welcomed Support, encouragement
Membership	Trusting Expressing warmth Seeing differences	Status seeking Need for role definition	Acceptance of nonconformity Trust and risk taking
Openness Data flow Decision making	Spontaneity Rapport Depth communication Disclosing	Strategy, caution Ambiguity Secrecy Distortion of data	Clarity, directness Spontaneous expression Listening, sharing Increasing feedback
Realization Goal formation Productivity	Asserting Exploring Clarifying own needs Achieving	Persuasion advice Extrinsic motivation Competition, rivalry Apathy, withdrawal	Involvement, creativity Cooperation Common goals Enthusiasm
Interdependence Control Organization	Participating Cooperating Giving and getting freedom	Dependency Bargaining Formal rules Structure, channels	Informality Flexible structures Little need for leaders Roles, power irrelevant

Adapted from Gibb, 1978.

In keeping with this humanistic orientation, the theory also expects the group worker (teacher, coach, supervisor) to be working on the same modal concerns as part of the group. As you noticed in the chart on TORI Group Development, a mature group has integrated the leadership/management function and does not need someone to organize, teach, manage, or supervise. The basic question for a worker using TORI theory is, "What would I be doing if I trusted this group more?" The following chart gives some suggestions.

TORI Group Leaders

Move Away from—TORI LEADERS—Move Toward

Move Away from	Move Toward
Doing what's helpful	Responding to my feelings
Modeling appropriate behaviors	Sharing all of me
Focus on motives and interpretations	Focus on experienced behavior now
Concern for them, past and future	Concern for now (being present)
Focus on limitations of each of us and what we need to get along	Focus on the strengths and growing edges of each of us
Managing the process	Getting into the process and flow
Planning, preparation, format	Focus on doing it

Adapted from Gibb, 1978.

Chapter 6

How to Observe Group Behavior

Group leadership is effective to the extent that it facilitates growth of the group and its task accomplishments. To be effective leaders and facilitators, we need to know what is going on in a group and select among our skills and resources accordingly. Direct observation is the most frequently used method to gather information about a group. Sharpening up our observation skills is a pretty sure way of making groups more effective. All of us are informal observers of the groups in which we participate and informally use our observations in our participation. We observe those areas that have become important to us through our many experiences and likely pay little attention to other areas. Sharpening up our observation skills consists of broadening the variety of areas we observe and then making our observations more systematic so that information from one meeting can be compared with similar data from other meetings. As observations are compared over a period of time, ups and downs in the group can be easily spotted and can be used for program evaluation and long-range planning.

Some kind of an observation guide or set of observation categories helps to make group observations more useful by clarifying which are the important areas or dynamics to watch and focusing the observer's attention on them. There are so many things to watch in a group that no one could accurately observe half of them, and even if teams of observers watched them all, it would take hours to summarize and process the data. Which areas to select is a judgment based on previous experience, but hopefully influenced by a review of suggested observation areas from the literature and the selection of some kind of framework or theory of group development. A guide also helps to make our observations more comprehensive and tends to balance out our tendency to neglect areas not important to us and to have one-sided views. A broadly focused guide sensitizes the observer to new areas of group interaction, thus checking their usefulness to the observer's frame of reference and intervention strategy.

What, then, is the most useful observation guide—the most important group dimensions to observe? After thirty years of working hard on this question (training, consulting, and research), my answer is a discouraging "it doesn't make a lot of difference which categories or frameworks are used as long as the guide makes sense to the observer and facilitates a comprehensive summary identifying priority areas for work and improvement." Certainly the information collected through observation is more useful if the observer has a clear picture of the priority dimensions of group growth, and this takes us back to reviewing the theories emerging from group research or a specific frame of reference that makes sense to us. Observation categories should emerge from our views of how groups grow and develop.

Observation is the most important method for gathering information about groups because everyone related to the groups is already doing it. With our goal of refining, focusing, broadening, and systemizing observations, it may be beneficial to explore the three major purposes of group observers. The first category is the *participant-observer* and includes everyone in the group (participants, leaders, staff workers) who is using observations to help figure out what is happening in the group and make the interventions of that person more useful. The second category includes the *training observer* or assigned group process observer whose goal is to help the whole group understand more about what is happening in the group and motivate them to appropriate action. In the *training observer* role, the importance of the quality of the data observed decreases, as the reporting skills of the observer more usually determine success. Typically, the process observer reports periodically through a group session or is given a chunk of time at the end of the session. The chief goal of the *training observer* is to gain acceptance for the data presentation process and stimulate further discussion and analysis of it by the group. This is facilitated by giving descriptive, non-judgmental data on the group and perhaps leaving it a bit open-ended to encourage other perspectives from the group. It is likely that these group feedback skills are harder to learn than those of basic group observation. The *program observer* role of the supervisor is the third category, and its goal is to evaluate the program to provide information for supervising the group worker, and future program planning. It is particularly important for program evaluation to have observations of predetermined, standardized areas to reduce observer bias and increase the comparability of several programs.

OBSERVATION TECHNIQUES

The concern about which observation guide to start using was reduced by saying that a particular category was less important than the regular use of some category related to a framework of group development. If in doubt, start with the Group Observation Guide (later in this chapter) which relates to most of the frameworks presented here. The next question is, "How should the observation be recorded?" Let me put this concern into perspective by saying that almost everyone collects much more data than can ever be used. In training process observers I start by having them cut in half whatever they had planned to observe.

In general, observations can be:

1. Put into predetermined categories (roles of group members).
2. Rated (survey of group development, behavior frequency observation guide).
3. Tabulated in numerical frequencies (how many times each member spoke).
4. Charted (who spoke to whom, who sat next to whom, who paired with whom for a task).
5. Described in anecdotes (John arrived ten minutes late for the meeting and sat down giggling).
6. Recorded in a running account.
7. Summarized in a narrative record. (See outline later in this section.)

As a participant observer or training observer, it is important that the observations and their recording doesn't get in the way of fairly full participation in the group. The observer can prepare for the task by looking the guide over before the session and becoming familiar with the categories or areas. For the first few times of its use, it is helpful to have the guide handy where it can be glanced over during the meeting or perhaps a note or two made on it. After the group session, the observer will take some time and complete recording with the guide.

An observation record will be most useful if it separates descriptions from hunches and interpretations. In my observation records, for example, I put my subjective observations and hunches in parentheses (members seem to be getting tired of discussing this issue), and my interpretations in brackets [the group seems determined not to let Marilyn take over the group again today]. Usually I have a lot of questions to myself and the group, and this, too, I separate by putting in parentheses (Libby is sure talking a lot—what's got her going?) and (why has this budget issue come up again—wasn't it resolved in the last meeting?).

Observers may also be concerned about how they should present their material—guide sheet, recording pages—to the group and describe their role. Opinions vary about how this is best done, but my strong view is that a straightforward, materials-on-the-table approach is most successful. Observers should briefly describe their interests in observing to the group and the areas they will be watching. When I am the observer, I also mention who will be reading my notes or how they will be used, and say that my notes can be read by members anytime. This serves as a convenient introduction to the group of the usefulness of process observations and may stimulate members to do more thoughtful observing themselves. Members will then be more ready to hear the observer's report, discuss it, and give their own observations about factors helping and hindering the work of the group.

If there is to be a training function for the group observer, the ideal situation is for the total group to work out the areas they want to have observed and either take turns being the observer or have a pair of observers who do it for several sessions (to get some continuity and comparisons in their observations), and then to pass the task on to a new pair. In my consulting or program evaluation work with groups, I describe my observation and recording functions and then ask for a volunteer who will join me as an inside observer. This has always worked well in my experience, as the observer who is a regular participant in the group usually has insights that I, as a newcomer, don't have. In any case, the more interest and involvement there is from members in the observation activity, the more likely the information generated will be accepted by the group and used in its action planning.

It is important for the observer to find ways of conducting observations without disrupting the group activity or separating himself or herself from the group. Research on this concern indicates that observing group behavior and making records does not affect the group's operation if the observer is able to establish rapport with the group. Members and staff usually have this rapport and new members can build it by demonstrating real interest in the group's success, tuning in to the group, and being open about how the observations will be used by the group and others.

My concerns are more about how much visibility and attention I, as an observer, want to get. If I am in a training observer function trying to motivate the whole group to spend more time and energy on process observation and feedback, I sit center stage (it's hard to observe if you can't see everyone in the group) and record on $8\frac{1}{2}$" x 11" pages attached to a clip board or in a looseleaf notebook. For situations where I want to minimize attention to my observing/recording function, I either jot occasional notes on 3" x 5" cards or write in a 4" x $6\frac{1}{2}$" looseleaf notebook I can slip in my back pocket.

The coming of inexpensive, yet powerful tape recorders and more recently, video cassette recorders, has brought a lot of use of this equipment to the group observation function. The assumption supporting electronic recording is that it reveals the group as it was and provides an unbiased record of proceedings. This hasn't been the case as straight sound recordings don't show body posture, nonverbal behavior, or even when participants leave the room and return. Video cameras are not able to take in all the group at once and the person at the camera must use his biases to decide what part of the action will be recorded. While recordings are useful for providing individuals with descriptive feedback, their effectiveness in replacing group observers has not been demonstrated. The time put into setting them up, operating them, and finding segments of interest to the group (few groups want to see their whole meeting again) and then figuring out what it means is rarely as useful to group action planning as a crisp, well-focused observer's report followed by a high-involvement group discussion. Personal growth, program evaluation, and research possibilities with recordings are another story and are discussed in the program evaluation guide.

One of the most useful contributions of recording a group session, especially with a small, unobtrusive cassette recorder, is in helping the observer improve the quality and accuracy of his or her records. Listening to the tape while looking over the observation record of the group's meeting provides the observer with an unusual opportunity to check out perceptions with the very objective, verbal record on the tape. If the observer missed any significant incident during the meeting this will show up in comparing the observation notes to the tape recording. Another method of improving observations is to have a team of observers, two or three people, who can compare their notes and pick up on any missed areas. In several of my projects we asked our visitors to take on an observation role with the regular observer and share perceptions. This usually made the session more interesting for the visitor and gave the group the benefit of some fresh insights. Later I set up "observation visitations" with teams of observers from parallel programs attending each other's sessions and reporting on their observations before they left.

The use of tape recordings and co-observers are especially useful as training aids for people just learning observation methods, but they are also useful in checking and validating information collected through observations. It is always a good practice to try to get three different viewpoints or sources of information to confirm a major conclusion. This triangulation to check accuracy would have a group observer look for two other sources of information such as the tape recording, a co-observer, informal interviews with the participants, program records of the group, written questionnaires or surveys from the participants, or diaries or records kept by other group members. In practice it is usually best to have two independent observers who check their perceptions with the group and follow up by informally interviewing the members after the meeting. If the quality of the information is still in doubt, a three- or four-question post-meeting reaction questionnaire should complete the triangulation and establish beyond reasonable doubt the validity of the information. This kind of validation increases in importance if the information is to be used for comparisons between or among groups or for agency program evaluation purposes.

Another group observation concern is the balancing of observation areas such as content and process. Content refers to what the group is working on and what it is saying, while process looks at how the group is working. This is the analogy to the "words and the music," where the words represent the overt task and concern of the group and the music reflects the real issues or concerns of the members (inclusion, control, intimacy) in working on these tasks. Over a period of time observers will want to get more "music" into their observations by looking at what people say and do and trying to get at its real intent or meaning. Often the words of participants, if taken at face value, do not reveal their intended communication: "I think Judi has a good idea here but. . ." (real meaning, "I disagree"). "I'd like to get some clarification of Gervase's idea; did he mean. . .?" (real meaning, "My opinion is. . ."). "Let me summarize the ideas presented to date" (one idea is given the spotlight which seems to be the idea with which the summarizer agrees). Or, if the group continues to flog a dead issue, the observer may feel it is flight to escape dealing with an intense, interpersonal conflict which has just surfaced. Member interactions should be taken as straightforwardly as possible, but if hunches or interpretations occur to the observer, they should be recorded, but clearly identified as hunches or interpretations (parentheses or brackets in my records).

In addition to balancing the observations of the content with the process, consideration should be given to balancing observations about individuals with those of the group as a whole. As excitement about an activity or issue increases, there is a tendency to watch the key players very carefully and sometimes miss what the low participants are doing, what they may be communicating through body language or nonverbal behavior, or what the overall mood of the group is during the excitement. Checking over an observation guide periodically or setting up time sampling helps to balance observations. And, there may even be a moment to note observations of what didn't happen.

TRAINING GROUP OBSERVERS

As usual, experiential training or "learning by doing" works best for training observers and basic training can start with making observations and then discussing what was observed with others at the close of the session. More sophisticated training often has observers in training looking over several observation guides, trying out the ones that look interesting in order to gain practice with a broad variety of observation areas, and discussing observations with other observers in training after each practice session. The practice sessions are usually real groups the trainees are working with, but may start with simulated group meetings within the training group. Observers work most effectively and accurately if they design their own observation guide or major areas to observe, and this activity should be facilitated within the training program. In my training programs our last activity is for each person to work out an observation plan for observing and reporting on a real group that I bring in for everyone to observe, and then comparing results with the other observers and getting feedback from the real group members.

A lot of group biases and value judgments are likely to appear during early practices. This is quite natural as most people quickly move their descriptive observations to a conclusion or evaluation so they can take action, and it takes considerable practice to record the descriptions first. Observers will report "the room was too smoky" rather than noting that three people asked if the smoking could be limited and another person opened the window. Or, the observer may report the setting was stimulating and appropriate rather than saying the group met in a library with the walls lined with books and the participants seated around a large rectangular table. In training sessions, observers pair up and exchange their observation reports. Each person identifies all the conclusions made by the other and asks for the descriptive data which led to making that conclusion. This practice is particularly valued after an observer finds that in reporting to a real group, the descriptions are always safe and lead to further discussion, while the conclusions may arouse resentment and close the group off from the observer.

OBSERVATION GUIDE—DEVELOPMENTAL AREAS

Observation guides are something like road maps in that they can save a lot of time and energy and keep people moving into relatively unknown areas from "driving in circles." Even very experienced drivers will consult a road map to figure out the most desirable route to their destination. Some will take the shortest route and conserve on energy consumption, others will take the fastest route figuring that time is money, and some prefer the scenic route or try to avoid major congested areas with other reasons in mind. In any case, after traveling the areas many times the road map may be checked periodically to make sure something isn't being missed but is usually put away. The following selection of guides and observation tools are very useful in exploring relatively new territory and checking from time to time that there aren't perhaps tougher but more productive pathways to group development available. In the long run they should be set aside as observers develop their own guides based on the specific needs and problems of the groups with whom they are working.

Following the sequence of viewpoints of group development presented in the last section, the first guide is set up to remind the observer of the points to look for under the five major areas of a group's operation. This guide is designed for the separate sheets to be placed in front of the observer, side by side. They may be stapled to a file folder and opened like a book which makes it a bit easier to handle them. Look at the guide that starts below and you will notice a number of different subquestions phrased in just a few words and leaving very little space for an extended answer. It is expected that the observer will glance over the guide sheets every little while during a meeting or activity and make a note or two of something that has become clear. Very little is written during the activity, but constantly thinking about these areas and making a few notes enable the worker to complete the record or write it up in a narrative fashion after the meeting. After the observer is familiar with the categories, he or she can participate with the group in the normal way and not be tied down to making more than a few notes with this guide sheet. Watching and participating in the group comes first, making notes second.

GROUP OBSERVATION GUIDE

A. CLIMATE

Physical setup conducive to interaction?	Distractions?	Ventilation, lighting
	Time limit (pressure) on space?	

Emotional climate cooperative/competitive	Formal-informal support?	Accepting/judgmental pride in group

Do members express feelings (fears, desires, concerns)?

B. INVOLVEMENT

Why are members here?   Lateness/absenteeism   Interest in group talk?

Stake in problem   Commitment to group?

Attentive (list who)   Restless   Withdrawn

C. INTERACTION

Lines of communication (one to one, one to group, or all through leader)

Distribution of participation (what percentage of group did half the talking?)
(Overparticipators)   (Underparticipators)

Who has the power in the group?   Pairings, subgroups

Impact of group size on interaction   Balance of task and group-building roles:

Are people listening and building   Task _____%
on the ideas of others?
    Group _____%

Group _____ Date _____ Time _____ Observer _____

D. COHESION

Degree of group solidarity   Group vs. individual interests

Group norms observed   Who doesn't conform?

What pressure on deviants
to conform?

Readiness to accept
majority decisions

E. PRODUCTIVITY

Are the goals clear?   Realistic?   Understood by all?

Were goals stated—did members contribute to statement?

Was there a flexible plan for reaching a goal? Understood by all? Followed?

Effectiveness of procedures and outcomes evaluated regularly?

What steps did group use in making decisions? Where did it get off track?

Were decisions from last session carried out?

Was next session planned? How?

Effect of leader/chairperson, chief executive or advisor, recorder/secretary roles?

Style of leadership?   Impact on participation? Where did it get to?

Notes on productivity during session

    Many of the questions raised in all five sections of the Group Observation Guide are appropriate ones to ask the group members or raise for discussion. "Were the problems we worked on today important ones to you?" "Why?" "Did you all understand our goal; what we were trying to accomplish?" "Did you feel any pressure to change your opinion and go along with the majority?" If this can be done it helps the worker check the observations.

Under the heading of *interaction* it is suggested that who speaks to whom is worth noting. Do the members usually talk to one or two people (the officers or the power figures); to the worker, to a best friend, or to everyone? If this guide is enlarged to an 8½″ x 11″ file folder size, there will be room for an interaction diagram (Figure 7) as it is often helpful to show the lines of communication. In this case, an additional page can be added for the interaction diagram and additional comments on roles of group members.

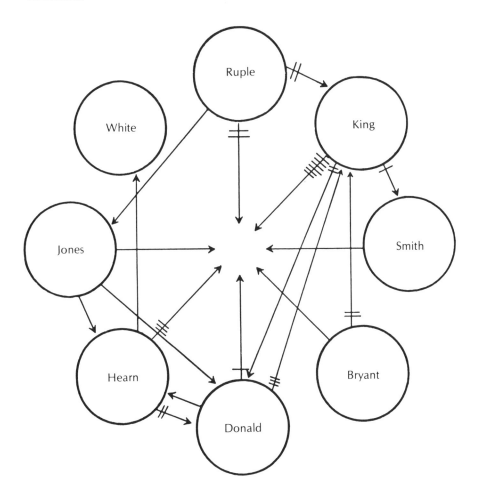

An interaction diagram of a small group based on two samples of five minutes each.

Figure 7

An interaction diagram also shows the diversity of participation and the amount of participation for each person. Two five-minute samples during an hour's meeting usually provide a reasonably accurate picture of interaction and it can be corrected and generalized from after the meeting with less precise observations made during the rest of the meeting. An easy form for showing interactions is illustrated in Figure 7. The arrow shows the person to whom the remarks were directed, or, if they are addressed to the total group, the arrow stops in the middle. The number of times a person talked is tabulated by counting the number of arrows he sends out, plus the number of dash marks on each of the arrows. In Figure 7, King spoke twelve times and White did not participate. During this part of the meeting the worker, who was observing, did not participate.

Appropriate group procedures are needed to facilitate decision making. The topics under structure and the effect of the chairperson's role in the guide suggest observation of the factors often directly related to the inefficient and frustrating problem-solving procedures of a group.

SURVEY OF GROUP DEVELOPMENT

The tool called "Survey of Group Development" was designed for intermittent use with a group. The observer or staff person would ordinarily complete this form after every few meetings and use it to chart the development of the group in these key areas. The tool has been used extensively by group participants as an aid to their assessing and analyzing their group operation. It is particularly useful for program evaluations and comparisons of programs in camps, social service, recreation, and informal educational programs. While the survey requires only thirteen check marks the average completion time is about twenty minutes.

Experience has shown that this survey is best completed following a group meeting or program activity, but the thirteen dimensions covered in the survey should be the focus for observations during the meeting. Some observers find it helpful to jot down the thirteen dimensions on 3" x 5" cards and glance over them during the meeting as a reminder.

As observers become more familiar with the thirteen dimensions and skilled in their observations related to them, they find the four choices for each area do not allow them to record their real assessments. At this point they should either modify the suggested descriptions by changing a word here and there, or write up their own summary under each of the headings.

Group_____ Date_____ Completed by_____

SURVEY OF GROUP DEVELOPMENT

For each area, place an X in the box which most nearly describes the group.

1. **UNITY** (Degree of unity, cohesion, or "we-ness.")

☐ Group is just a collection of individuals or sub-groups; little group feeling.

☐ Group is very close and there is little room or felt need for other contacts and experience.

☐ Some group feeling. Unity stems more from external factors than from real friendship.

☐ Strong common purpose and spirit based on real friendships. Group usually sticks together.

2. **SELF-DIRECTION** (The group's own motive power.)

☐ Little drive from anywhere, either from members or worker.

☐ Domination from a strong single member, a clique, or the worker.

☐ Group has some self-propulsion but needs considerable push from worker.

☐ Initiation, planning, executing, and evaluating comes from total group.

3. **GROUP CLIMATE** (The extent to which members feel free to be themselves.)

☐ Climate inhibits good fun, behavior, and expression of desire, fears, and opinions.

☐ Members freely express needs and desires; joke, tease, and argue to detriment of the group.

☐ Members express themselves but without observing interests of total group.

☐ Members feel free to express themselves but limit expression to total group welfare.

4. **DISTRIBUTION OF LEADERSHIP** (The extent to which leadership roles are distributed among members.)

☐ A few members always take leader roles. Rest are passive.

☐ Many members take leadership but one or two are continually followers.

☐ Some of the members take leader roles but many remain passive followers.

☐ Leadership is shared by all members of the group.

5. **DISTRIBUTION OF RESPONSIBILITY** (The extent to which responsibility is shared among members.)

☐ Everyone tries to get out of jobs.

☐ Many members accept responsibilities but do not carry them out.

☐ Responsibility carried by a few members.

☐ Responsibilities are distributed among and carried out by nearly all members.

6. **PROBLEM SOLVING** (Group's ability to think straight, make use of everyone's ideas, and decide creatively about its problems.)

☐ Not much thinking as a group. Decisions made hastily, or group lets leader or worker do most of the thinking.

☐ Some thinking as a group but not yet an orderly process.

☐ Some cooperative thinking but group gets tangled up in pet ideas of a few. Confused movement toward solutions.

☐ Good pooling of ideas and orderly thought. Everyone's ideas are used to reach final plan.

7. **METHOD OF RESOLVING DISAGREEMENTS WITH GROUP** (How does group work out disagreements?)

☐ Group follows lead of leader or waits for the worker to resolve disagreements.

☐ Compromises are effected by each subgroup giving up something.

☐ Strongest subgroup dominates through a vote and majority rule.

☐ Group as a whole arrives at a solution that satisfies all members and that is better than any single suggestion.

8. **MEETS BASIC NEEDS** (The extent to which group gives a sense of security, achievement, approval, recognition, and belonging.)

☐ Group experience adds little to the meeting of most members' needs.

☐ Group experience contributes substantially to basic needs of most members.

☐ Group experience contributes to some degree to basic needs of most members.

☐ Group contributes substantially to basic needs of all members.

9. **VARIETY OF ACTIVITIES**

☐ Little variety in activities—stick to same things.

☐ Considerable variety in activities. Try out new activities.

☐ Some variety in activities.

☐ Great variety in activities. Continually trying out new ones.

10. **DEPTH OF ACTIVITIES** (The extent to which activities are gone into in such a way that members can use full potentialities, skills, and creativity.)

☐ Little depth in activities—just scratching the surface.

☐ Considerable depth in activities. Members able to utilize some of their abilities.

☐ Some depth but members are not increasing their skills.

☐ Great depth in activities. Members find each a challenge to develop their abilities.

11. **WORKER-MEMBER RAPPORT** (Relations between the group and the worker; percent who are:)

☐ Antagonistic or resentful.

☐ Friendly and interested. Attentive to worker's suggestions.

☐ Indifferent toward worker. Friendship neither sought nor rejected. Noncommunicative.

☐ Intimate relations: openness and sharing. Strong rapport.

12. **ROLE OF THE WORKER** (The extent to which the group is centered around the worker.)

☐ Activities, discussion, and decisions revolve around interests, desires, and needs of worker.

☐ Worker acts as stimulator—suggests ideas or other ways of doing things. Helps group find ways of making own decisions.

☐ Group looks to worker for suggestions and ideas. Worker decides, when member gets in a jam.

☐ Worker stays out of discussion and makes few suggestions of things to do. Lets members carry the ball themselves.

13. **STABILITY**

☐ High absenteeism and turnover; influences group a great deal.

☐ Some absenteeism and turnover with minor influence on group.

☐ High absenteeism and turnover; little influence on group growth.

☐ Low absenteeism rate and turnover. Group very stable.

However, if the survey is to be used for measurement and comparison purposes, modifications of the descriptions are not appropriate and observers should go back to selecting that box which most nearly describes the group. Comparisons of these critical areas of a group's development over a period of time provide a rather accurate measurement of a group's growth as well as an indicator of group health and usefulness for program evaluation. It may seem that this survey is subject to observer judgment or bias, yet our research has shown that independent observers have a high interobserver reliability (significant at .05 level) and that ratings by members, workers, and supervisors correlate at the same high level of significance.

ROLES OF GROUP MEMBERS

This is one of the most popular observation tools as it encourages descriptions of individual behavior and makes for specific feedback to each member. Leadership training groups find practicing different roles and getting feedback on the practice very useful in developing a larger repertoire of roles and gaining skill and comfort in when to use them. Groups trying to increase their effectiveness will have the observer focus on the total group (not identifying individual roles) and perhaps show a frequency chart to illustrate the overplayed roles and the ones rarely taken that the group might want to work at adding.

To make a complete record of a meeting using this guide is a full-time job and removes the observer from participating. To be a participant-observer, time samples can be used for intensive recording. A five-minute sample every fifteen or twenty minutes works out pretty well. It is best if the time samples are determined ahead of time to increase the likelihood of their being a cross-section of the total meeting. Observing the roles of group members compliments video recording of a group, as both forms of observation make for specific feedback to individuals. This activity is particularly useful for training purposes where the goal is personal learning and skill development for individual members such as group dynamics classes, leadership and management training, and personal growth groups.

Let us now look at a couple of technical problems that come up in using this observation guide. More than one role is often taken as a participant speaks and it is difficult to decide how to categorize the input. A person may start off seeming to agree and build on a previous speaker's idea but ends up making a new proposal. Is this to be categorized as "supporting-encouraging " or "gives opinions"? While it is possible to list this contribution under both categories, my rule of thumb is to list it under the chief message it left with the group. In this case "gives opinions," as a new proposal, has more impact than some general agreement. Thus, "I am in general agreement with Noela's proposal, which I think this group has the resources to implement, yet I wonder if we might not do better having our own presentation and display two or three weeks later" (gives opinions). Or, a question may be followed with a new proposal. "Why do some members want to have us attend city council and propose that they assist us with some special funding? Wouldn't we be better off with a major story in the newspaper or on local television?" (gives opinions). If in doubt, the observer could list them under both categories and in the long run the group profile of roles would look pretty much the same.

ROLES OF GROUP MEMBERS DEFINITION SHEET

TASK FUNCTIONS

1. **Defines problems**—group problem is defined: overall purpose of group is outlined.
2. **Seeks information**—requests factual information about group problem or methods of procedure, or for clarification of suggestions.
3. **Gives information**—offers facts or general information about group problem, methods to be used, or clarifies a suggestion.
4. **Seeks opinions**—asks for the opinions of others relevant to discussion.
5. **Gives opinions**—states beliefs or opinions relevant to discussion.
6. **Tests feasibility**—questions reality, checks practicality of suggested solutions.

GROUP BUILDING AND MAINTENANCE FUNCTIONS

7. **Coordinating**—a recent statement is clarified and related to another statement in such a way as to bring them together. Proposed alternatives are reviewed.
8. **Mediating-harmonizing**—interceding in disputes or disagreements and attempting to reconcile them. Highlights similarities in views.
9. **Orienting-facilitating**—keeps group on the track, points out deviations from agreed-upon procedures or from direction of group discussion. Helping group process along, proposing other procedures to make group more effective.
10. **Supporting-encouraging**—expressing approval of another's suggestion, praising others' ideas, being warm and responsive to ideas of others.
11. **Following**—going along with the movement of the group, accepting ideas of others, expressing agreement.

INDIVIDUAL FUNCTIONS

12. **Blocking**—interfering with the progress of the group by arguing, resisting, and disagreeing beyond reason. Or, by coming back to same "dead" issue later.
13. **Out of field**—withdrawing from discussion, daydreaming, doing something else, whispering to others, leaving room, etc.
14. **Digressing**—getting off the subject, leading discussion in some "personally oriented direction," or making a brief statement into a long nebulous speech.

It is more difficult to categorize an intervention when the true meaning is given a verbal camouflage, especially if it is a fairly long speech. While the content of the intervention should be taken at face value and categorized accordingly, my rule of thumb is that when in doubt either list it as giving opinions or just omit it from the record. Often, the tendency for a new observer is to puzzle over the intervention for a bit and by then the next

ROLES OF GROUP MEMBERS

Put initials of each member at top of each column.

TASK ROLES										
Defines problem										
Seeks information										
Gives information										
Seeks opinions										
Gives opinions										
Tests feasibility										
GROUP BUILDING AND MAINTENANCE ROLES										
Coordinating										
Mediating-harmonizing										
Orienting-facilitating										
Supporting-encouraging										
Following										
INDIVIDUAL ROLES										
Blocking										
Out of field										
Digressing										

If a general, rather than individual, picture of the group is desired, the first column can be used to show the total times that function was taken by any group member. This would then show what functions were being overplayed and underplayed in the group.

speaker may say something that influences the rating. For example, if Tom rambles on and it is not clear whether he is supporting a previous idea, giving information about it, or seeking others' opinions about it and the next speaker says, "Yes, I, too, agree that this would make sense and that we should do it", there may be an influence to categorize Tom as giving opinions (agreement) or supporting-encouraging. The rule of thumb here is to try not to be influenced by a following statement in categorizing the previous one.

OTHER OBSERVATION AREAS

A number of other observation areas are listed as follows which the interested worker may want to use "cafeteria-style" in picking out additional categories to look at or in starting from scratch to build his own observation guide. The items are in no particular order and are in addition to the areas mentioned in the previous guide sheets though there is some overlapping.

1. Group rules (standards)—procedures for handling routines, dealing with absences, lateness, poor completion of jobs assigned, etc.
2. Clarity of members in expressing ideas.
3. How does the worker handle group problems?
4. Does the worker show favoritism among members?
5. List the members according to their status in the group.
6. How sensitive is the worker to the needs and interests of the members?
7. Method of control used by group.
8. Methods of resolving differences used by group.
9. Nonverbal communication/gestures (nodding head, tapping fingers), facial expressions (bored, surprised, disgusted), posture and position in relation to group.
10. Seating arrangement—who sits next to whom, who sits or participates on the fringe of the group, who is always centrally located, who often leaves group.
11. Who talks after whom (and what kind of reply is made?).
12. Critical incidents during activity.
13. Tension release through exuberant laughter or horseplay.
14. List position of members on controversial topic and identify subgroups and pairing.
15. How well was the program planned?

16. Use of available resources outside group (agency, community).
17. Leadership of worker—democratic versus autocratic; permissive versus restrictive.
18. Respect and regard for facilities and equipment.
19. Hidden agenda.
20. Invisible committees.
21. Pressures for and against making a decision.
22. Stressing of pride in the group.
23. Setting clear and attainable goals.
24. Arranging goals and work methods so that the group succeeds.
25. Helping each member to be aware of his or her contribution to group success.

The guide on the next page, like the Roles of Group Members Definition Sheet, is most useful in groups where indicators of the growth of individual members are needed or in training and personal development groups where feedback on individual behavior is appropriate. Consequently, this format has been used extensively in alternative educational programs for youth, camp groups, classrooms, growth groups, and in leadership and management training. Typically, two or three members volunteer to complete the observation guide, or it may be used by the staff person and outside observer in a program evaluation project. The specific observational areas described in the guide may be revised to focus on the actual goals and objectives of the groups under study. This guide is most useful when it is completed by more than one observer over a fair length of time in which several ratings have been made.

GROUP RECORDS

Group workers or process observers keep records of the growth of their groups in order to help the group grow and use the full potential of its members. As the worker gathers data from the observation guides and in the additional data collection methods described in Part 3 she puts much of it down in the group records to help her analyze the group's situation and plan procedures for helping it to move forward. These records form the basis for any kind of systematic or planned group development. They may also be used to measure the results of the group experience for its members, provide information for annual reports and interpretive statements of the

BEHAVIOR FREQUENCY OBSERVATION GUIDE

Group _____ Observer _____ Date of rating _____

Rate the frequency of
each person's behavior using

0 = not observed

1 = once or twice

2 = a few times

3 = frequently

1. Initiated activities							
2. Assumed leadership in group							
3. Made friendly approaches to others							
4. Withdrawn or out of group							
5. Got angry and shouted or sulked							
6. Showed vim and enthusiasm for activity							
7. Showed off, boasted, sought attention							
8. Disrupted or disturbed group							
9. Fidgeted, twitched, appeared nervous							
10. Helped others to participate or learn							
11. Helped group to evaluate its performance							
12. Praised or supported others							

agency, and help to orient a new worker to the group in the future. Group records provide a basis for supervision that is focused on helping the worker understand the group and improve its effectiveness in achieving the organization's goals. The major records for the worker to keep include: Survey of Group Development (the major dimensions of group growth), Behavior Frequency Observation Guide (major value dimensions of individual growth), and Survey of Member Activity. These three are supplemented by more extensive group observation records as described here, and by the sociometric measures, member and parent ratings, interest finders, member reactions, and other personal data described in Part 3.

Two other forms of records have not been mentioned: anecdotal records and narrative descriptions. Essentially, an anecdotal record describes in purely objective terms an interesting or unusual event that happened either to an individual, a subgroup, or the total group. Areas to consider for the possible writing of anecdotes have been described under observation headings; the major difference is the method of recording. The job of the recorder is to select incidents worth reporting and describe them objectively. These incidents should describe a wide range of behavior, both positive and negative, of individuals in the group and of total group behavior. Single incidents do not have much meaning but as the anecdotes accumulate, they have real value as they present an over-a-period-of-time, objective set of descriptions which can be used for diagnostic and comparative purposes. One of the best things about anecdotal records is that as they are brief descriptions of something that happened, people who were not part of the group can read them and make independent judgments about what was going on. These outside "judges" may be classmates, other agency staff or supervisors, and their role is to help the observer check out possible bias by giving an independent summary or analysis of what they think is going on in the group. This approach is part of the triangulation method of increasing the accuracy of observation information by trying to get three different views of an event or group characteristic. Procedures for using judges' ratings of anecdotal records for measurement and program evaluation are described in the Program Evaluation guide.

Anecdotes should be dated to establish their sequence in time and the setting or activity of the group should be mentioned to put the description in context. Identifying the noise, lack of concentration, and silly antics of a group comes into perspective only if it is recorded that it was the evening of the last day of school for the year. Each anecdote should be reported in a factual, objective way. Value judgments or interpretations by the recorder are best omitted unless they are necessary to make the picture clear.

Examples of useful anecdotes:

- In the club meeting today the group discussed plans for their Christmas party and which girls they would invite. Pierre did not participate in the discussion. He fidgeted in his chair and wiggled his fingers. He was the first to leave at the close of the meeting.

- As the group came back from the ballfield after losing the game the boys became more and more quiet. Finally, after a period of silence, Hank said, "We should have won the damn game anyway." Tears streaked down his cheek. George and Tom wept a little, too.

- The eleven members of the board sat around a large table in low chairs and each member had a thick folder of papers in front of her. After opening the meeting, Libby (chair) asked members to get out the consultants' report on revitalizing the association. It took three or four minutes for everyone to find the document in her large collection of papers. Libby made several attempts to start the discussion but couldn't get going until all had found the document.

Narrative or descriptive records are kept in diary form with the worker describing what happened and how he or she felt and reacted to these happenings. These records are usually written shortly after the time span to be reported on (a meeting or a day at camp) has elapsed. Figure 8 gives an outline of the kind of descriptions that should be included in a narrative record. Added to this is the basic information about the group, names of those present, time and place of the meeting, setting of the meeting, and other conditions affecting the meeting (weather, holiday, exam period, etc.). The focus of the narrative record is on the group process—how members reacted to one another and to the worker—and not as much on the program content. The major weakness of narrative records is the time involved in writing them up, but this can be considerably reduced by tape recording the narrative description (small cassette recorders are best), and having a stenographer type up the records.

Records are an accepted part of systematic group work and of educational supervision, but the question raised by many students and beginning workers is "What records should I keep?" The most honest answer is "Those records that will help you to work with the group more effectively in order that it can achieve its goals and the agency's goals." But this is not very helpful.

There is no general answer as the background and training of the worker and the unique aspects of the group make a great deal of difference. Volunteer workers with little professional background will want simple, straightforward records that will gradually increase their understanding. Advanced professional workers doing intensive work or research will want complete records combining most of the material described herein.

My own opinion has been to encourage workers in the many different organizations where I have worked or been a consultant to use three surveys (Survey of Group Development, either of the individual surveys—Roles of Group Members or Behavior Frequency Observation Guide, and Survey of Member Activity) as the basic records and to supplement these with other information, especially friendship finders or social relations indexes, as the situation appears to warrant it. In settings where there is a major emphasis on educational supervision, the narrative record is very useful for the workers' growth, as it allows the workers to describe things in their own words and is more flexible than check-off sheets. Our rule continues to be not collecting more data than we can use, but trying to expand our resources and develop our skills wherever possible.

REPORTING OBSERVATIONS TO YOUR GROUP

There is a great challenge in reporting observations to your group in your role as a *participant-observer* or training observer that has more to do with the way you present your material than with the quality of your material. Groups like to feel that their observer, or anyone helping to process group experiences, is working on an assignment by the group and responsible to the group for that task. It is a service role much like the group recorder who makes a report on the content of the group's meetings and looks for additions and corrections. The excitement of the observer role and the opportunity to watch individual roles and overall group operation makes it easy to move to a judgmental or evaluative stance in reporting group observations. This tends to distance the observer from the group by setting him or her up as an evaluator who tells the group, and individuals, what has been going wrong. The group may react by rejecting the observer's report actively—that is, arguing against it. Or, they may reject it passively by politely thanking the observer and then quickly going on to the next item of business. After two or three such experiences the group finds it "doesn't have time" for the observer's report and looking at the group's process becomes a low priority and gradually disappears as a group activity.

Groups that have continuing success with an observer function usually share it around the group with each member taking turns to report on from one to four group meetings. In an effort to move the observer's report from a lecture on what the group did that was helpful and not helpful, many groups either assign two observers or expect everyone to be a *participant-observer* and turn the observer report into a group discussion with many participants sharing their perception of what happened at the meeting and how it felt for them. As I mentioned earlier, when I am the *training observer* or the *program observer* (research observer) I enlist a group member to join me in the observer role, as this helps to get a member perspective on group process and it encourages other members to participate in the discussion of the observers' report.

As an observer it is helpful if you make a few provocative observations of key areas of the group's process in a descriptive rather than interpretive or judgmental fashion. Think of yourself as announcing a hockey game on the radio, describing as accurately as possible the key plays in the game with enough animation to keep all your listeners on the edge of their seats. Too much data, even if it is accurate and of high quality, is boring and counter-productive. Your goal is to present a crisp, yet comprehensive report that is tantalizing and will provoke members to respond in a general discussion.

This provocative stage is furthered if you present your observations in a descriptive way and then raise a number of questions about them. If you are prone to make interpretations try to make two or three possible inter-pretations of the same event so that others can join in trying to figure out what was happening and why. Or, try to pose your interpretations as hunches or questions—"Estelle was very emotional in her participation to-day and I wonder if that was related to what was going on in the group or something outside the group." "Irene made a number of interventions today that tried to keep us on track and accomplishing our tasks of recruiting new members—I'm not sure if this was an important task for her or if she just wanted to complete it as quickly as possible." "Dirk, Bob, and Sylvia raised a number of issues today about the use of our Planned Programming Budget System but I wasn't sure if they were meant to help us use the process more effectively or were designed to question our continued use of the PPBS approach." "The group seemed to be very lighthearted tonight and I don't know if it was related to the difficulty of the task or just a reflec-tion that this is our first board meeting in a while when we haven't had a very heavy agenda." The role of the observer is to provide data that the group can use to increase its effectiveness, and the more the group can iden-tify with the data and get excited by it the more likely it is to be used in group planning. The group maturity profile is a tool the observer can use to report observations and also stimulate group discussion of the observations.

Group _____ Date _____ Worker _____

SURVEY OF GROUP ACTIVITY

1. Briefly describe what the group did:

2. General reaction of the group and individuals to these activities:

3. How did the group plan? How were decisions made or activities decided on?

4. Description of group relationships (subgrouping or pairing, dependency, conflict, power plays, use of group pressure, group building):

5. Description of individual's behavior (cooperative, out of field, seeking attention— anything unusual or a problem):

The group maturity profile was designed to stimulate a discussion with a group about its stage of development. Typically, thirty or forty minutes would be set aside to assess where the group was in its development and how the members felt about how the group was doing. Each member of the group would be given a profile sheet and after a brief explanation of the four task stages and the four relationship stages, asked to rate the group on each of the two continuums. Responses could be located at any of four identified stages or partway between any two. Lines are then drawn from the horizontal and vertical ratings to the intersecting group development and productivity line and where they join indicates the maturity level or development phase of the group (indicated in the profile as low—medium— high). Members do individual ratings and then compare results. The facilitator of this group assessment activity may want to record perceptions

GROUP MATURITY PROFILE

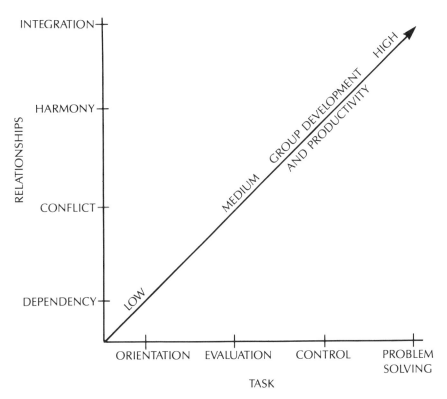

on a chalkboard or flip chart so that all viewpoints can be looked at together and some sort of group average can be charted. Looking at the data is usually quite provocative and leads to a useful analysis of where the group is and how members are feeling about what is happening. The background for the four stages of task development and relationship building is presented in the viewpoints of group development in Chapter 5.

TYPES OF DESCRIPTIONS
A NARRATIVE RECORD SHOULD CONTAIN

1. A description of the setting, who was present, and what the group did.
   A. A description of activities (*what* the group did).
   B. A description of feelings and emotions around the activities (*how* they did it).
   C. A description of how the activities came into being (member planning session, spontaneous, agency planned, etc.).

2. A description of the group's planning process. (This should tell not just what was discussed, but how the group planned and how decisions were reached.)

3. A description of how the members functioned as a group.
   A. Degree of cohesiveness (unity versus cliques, conflicts and individual behavior).
   B. Distribution of task-responsibility roles (few, some, or all) and how these roles were decided on (took turns, volunteered, appointed, etc.).

4. A description of individual members in the group.
   A. Group adjustment.
      1. Analysis of acceptance by group.
      2. Typical roles in group interaction (leadership, responsibility, nonfunctional behavior, individual roles).
      3. Typical roles in group planning.
   B. Participant learning or skill development (these may be technical skills—learned to make copper ashtray) or human relations skills (learned to accept wise remarks from others).
   C. Individual behavior.

5. Role of worker in group life. Description of:
   A. Areas of direction and control.
   B. Areas of limit setting and endorsing.
   C. Areas of stimulating and suggesting.
   D. Areas of showing technical know-how (how to make a bed roll or play a game).
   E. Areas of facilitating (helping things to come about).
   F. Use of relationships to influence individual behavior (modeling).

6. Relation of group to other groups, the agency, or the community.

Figure 8

REFERENCES AND BIBLIOGRAPHY

Bennis, Warren G. Patterns and vicissitudes in T-group development. In L. Bradford and others, eds., *T-group Theory and Laboratory Method.* New York: Wiley, 1963, pp. 248-278.

Bion, W.R. *Experiences in Groups.* New York: Basic Books, 1961.

Gibb, Jack R. *Trust: A New Theory of Personal and Organizational Development.* Los Angeles: Guild of Tudors Press, 1978.

Hare, A. Paul. *Handbook of Small Group Research* (2nd Edition). New York: Free Press, 1976.

Henry, Sue. *Group Skills in Social Work.* Itasca, IL: Peacock, 1981.

McGrath, Joseph. *Groups: Interaction and Performance.* Englewood Cliffs, NJ: Prentice-Hall, 1984.

Napier, Rodney and Matti Gershenfeld. *Groups: Theory and Experience* (2nd Edition). Boston: Houghton-Mifflin, 1981.

Patton, Michael Q. *Qualitative Evaluation Methods.* Beverly Hills, CA: Sage, 1980.

Schutz, William C. *FIRO—A Three Dimensional Theory of Interpersonal Behavior.* Reprinted as *The Interpersonal Underworld.* Palo Alto, CA: Science and Behavior Books, 1966.

Shaw, Marvin E. *Group Dynamics* (2nd Edition). New York: McGraw-Hill, 1981.

Zander, Alvin. *Making Groups Effective.* San Francisco: Jossey-Bass, 1982.

Part 3:
How to Analyze and
Evaluate Group Growth

Chapter 7

Collecting Group Information

Direct observation is the most frequently used, and most important, method of gathering information about a group. Yet, self-reports and assessments by others provide useful and exciting descriptions. These latter methods include program locators and interest finders, diaries, personal inventories, member nominations, reputation ratings, and surveys of parents or friends. They are particularly helpful in analyzing individual and group growth as they are somewhat more accurate than observations, which tend to be lopsided, as people tend to notice and remember those behaviors most important to them. And, they provide confirmation or fresh data with which to reassess the information and group diagnosis based on observational data.

Systematic observation usually gives a general picture of member roles and positions in a group and a nomination or peer rating technique is used to refine this general picture and increase its accuracy at the same time. Member nominations can confirm hunches based on observations (the triangulation approach) and they are very accurate predictors of what is going to happen in the group. The best way to understand individual behavior and relationships is to ask the group members to report on their needs and interests, attitudes and beliefs, and attraction to other group members. If a staff worker or group observer wants to check out observations about who has power and influence in the group, the best way is to ask the members.

When it comes to knowing what's going on in a group, what the potential of various members is, and which individuals are having a good or bad experience, the staff worker typically knows more than any other member but not as much as all the members together know. Thus, training cadets are more able to predict future leaders than their staff officers, students can identify other students with mental health problems more accurately than teachers, and sensitivity training participants can determine who will

require psychiatric help after the experience better than the staff facilitator. Self-descriptions and reports or nominations by others provide
remarkable insights about a group. Their accuracy and reliability encourage their use in evaluating group growth.

PEER NOMINATIONS AND SOCIOGRAMS

In diagnosing the strengths of a group and the likely blockages to effective
working relations, it is quite productive to analyze the relationships of
group members. Understanding these relationships helps predict how
interventions directed toward individuals will affect the group climate.
How individuals will act in a group is influenced by the values and
standards that the group sets and the individual's role or status in the
group. Included members seeking additional acceptance in a group behave
rather differently than fringe members resisting inclusion. The social status
or sociometric position of an individual is best established through a group
nomination technique.

Using this technique, members may be asked to nominate the three
people they would most like to work with on a committee. The number of
times a person is nominated shows that person's acceptance or social status
in the group. Checking on reciprocal choices (two people who nominate
each other) helps to identify small groups of friends or subgroups that in
turn determine the integration or cohesion of a group. Peer nominations
are usually charted on a graphic display and the completed display is called
a sociogram. A quick glance at the group's sociogram shows the extent of
subgroups, connections or cleavages among members, and the overall
togetherness of the members. The sociogram also shows the relative acceptance of members and can be used to establish the group's status hierarchy.

Peer nominations can also be used by group workers or team supervisors to help form new groups or put together temporary task groups. Team-
building activities within a work group usually involve peer descriptions
as a way of helping members understand the group's dynamics and the role
and function of each member in relationship to the group task (see, for example, the Dimock-Scott Interpersonal Skills Questionnaire later in this
chapter). Sociograms are also helpful in identifying members with interpersonal relations problems who may need special assistance.

How to Collect Sociometric Choices

The first task is to decide what it is you want the nominations to illustrate: acceptance or popularity, power, expertise or competence in some area, leadership, influence, or whatever. Assuming you want to construct a friend-ship chart for a youth group, you could gather the group together and hand members pencils and paper and ask them to list their three best friends in the group. Many youth and especially adults would feel self-conscious in doing this, wondering if the people they choose will choose them. It might feel like the old high school dance where the boys line up on one side and the girls on the other—then move to the middle to choose partners. Or, choos-ing up sides for a team activity where some individuals are over-chosen and others are completely left out. Depending, then, on the comfort level in the group and the possible anxiety about the nomination criteria, private listing of choices where members can feel anonymous may be in order. If this is not practical then the worker should try to establish a comfortable climate, eliminate side talk and horseplay during the process, and build in an ex-citing activity at the end of the process to divert members' focus and cut down on them telling each other about their choices.

The nomination technique is most meaningful if the focus of the ques-tion(s) has some valid and practical application such as members of a pro-ject group, car companions for a trip, a chairperson or captain of the group, tent mates for a hike, or representatives for a national committee.

In August most of us will be attending the national convention held this year in Niagara Falls. In order to help arrange transportation, please list the three people with whom you would most like to ride. While you won't get exactly who you choose, it will assist us in doing a better job of assigning seats.

My first choice is _____

My second choice is _____

My third choice is _____

(Nominations based on friendship)

It is not always possible for a worker to arrange some activity on the basis of group choices (though the possibilities seem endless) and "imag-ined" events can be used. "Who would you pick to go with you to the movies?" "Who would you want to take over during the counselor's day

Think back over the last few meetings of our board of directors and some of the decisions we have made. Then, list below three people who have most frequently influenced your thinking.

The three people are: _____

_____, and_____
(Nominations based on influence)

off?" "Who would you pick to take the chair if the president was absent?" "Who would you like to be captain of your team if we played another group in baseball?" Now, not all of these questions are asking the same thing and people are likely to respond to them with different names. The person selected for captain of the baseball team may be the best athlete rather than a best friend. The person picked to paddle a canoe may be a stronger paddler who will help to keep the canoe out in front of the others, rather than a best friend. And, the selection of a person to represent a group at an agency meeting may be the most responsible person or the most persuasive and this person again may not be a best friend. If the question is directly related to friendship such as bunk mate, seating companion, or hiking partner, one question will likely be enough to show friendship relationships. However, if the question contains other variables such as skill and personality which may influence the choice away from actual friends, it is better to ask two or three such questions and prepare three sets of data. Each friendship chart or sociogram should show the criteria used as the basis for selection. If it has been suggested that the results will be used to form groups for certain activities, the worker should now follow through and do the best job possible to arrange the groups on the basis of the choices. If some members have been left out they can be put in with those that they choose although this, in many cases, will mean that the others will be with their second or, perhaps, third choices instead of their first choices. It is usually better to include the isolates in this way in order that they can begin to become integrated in the group rather than give the first choices to the over-chosen members of the group who are, after all, the most secure.

There is no definite number of friendship choices that should be asked for and research on this point varies a great deal. The rule of thumb in our research has been to ask for three choices if the group is less than fifteen in number, and to ask for five choices if the group numbers more than fifteen. If the question asks the member to list choices both within and outside of the group, ten choices may be asked for and this has worked out quite well, as long as the subjects are ten years of age or older.

In some situations it may be of interest to the worker to compare the results from one group with other groups. This can be very enlightening, especially for the worker who is responsible for leading or supervising these groups, but care must be taken to use the same criteria, ask for the same number of choices, and ask the questions to the groups at about the same time.

One of the variables that should be considered in larger groups who make their choices in the presence of one another is the physical presence of all members of the group at that time. Teenagers, and especially younger youth, tend to leave out of their choices the absent members unless they are reminded of who's absent or their names are put on a chalkboard. When the members of a large group are being questioned individually, the worker may want to provide a complete list of member names in order that each individual will have the same exposure to all the names together.

How to Construct a Friendship Chart

After the friendship choices have been collected from all the members of the group, the worker prepares a chart (Figure 9) on which to tabulate and diagram the choices. Figure 9 was designed for small groups of not more than eight members. Figures 10 and 11 are for larger groups. Two group members are included in Figure 12 to show how the information is put on the chart.

Friendship patterns in a group often become more clear if, in completing the diagram in the lower half of Figure 9, the first choices of everyone are put in first, then all the second choices, and finally the third. Between each round the worker can pause and get a picture of the group at a different level. Some boys receive no first choices but several second choices and this is highlighted in the three-step process.

FRIENDSHIP CHART
(In-group choices)

First choice   = 5
Second choice = 3
Third choice   = 2

Group Advisor _____Scudder_____

Group _____Anzacks_____

Date_____May 2nd_____

Criteria for choices ___Sleep mates___

CHOSEN

	1. Ruple	2. King	3. Smith	4. Bryant	5. Donald	6.	7.	8.
Last Names								
1. Ruple		5	3	2				
2. King	2		3		5			
3. Smith								
4. Bryant								
5. Donald								
Totals								

CHOOSERS

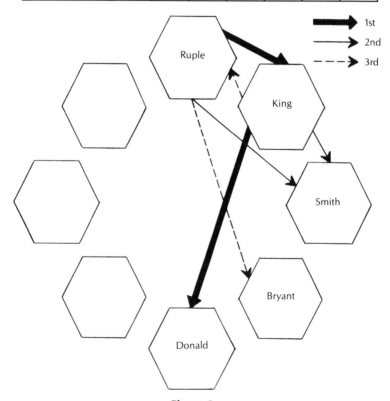

1st
2nd
3rd

Ruple
King
Smith
Bryant
Donald

Figure 9

FRIENDSHIP CHART
(In-group choices)

Date _____   Worker_____

Criteria for choices _____   Group _____

Weight for 3 choices   **Weight for 5 choices**
  1st = 5   1st = 9   4th = 4
  2nd = 3   2nd = 7   5th = 3
  3rd = 2   3rd = 5

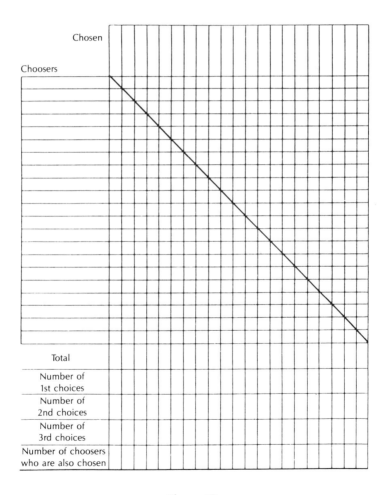

Figure 10

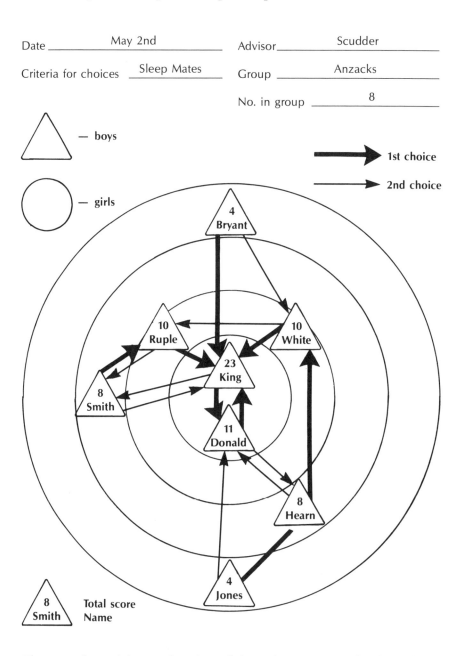

The scores for each boy are based on all three choices (5, 3, and 2) but only the first two choices are shown on the sociogram.

Figure 11

Your name _____Grant Ruple_____	Your name _____Bob King_____
List below the three boys in our group you would most like to have sleep next to you at our next night out.	List below the three boys in our group you would most like to have sleep next to you at our next night out.
First choice _____Bob King_____	First choice _____Phil Donald_____
Second choice _____Tom Smith_____	Second choice _____Tom Smith_____
Third choice _____Joe Bryant_____	Third choice _____Grant Ruple_____

Figure 12

For a larger group the chart in the upper half of Figure 9 can be expanded and five choices can be shown. Figure 10 is set up in this way.

Many workers ask the basis of the weighting of the first, second, and third choices. Is one first choice really more than two third choices? The answer is that the weighting of scores is purely arbitrary and the scores assigned the different choices have merely been the ones that the co-researchers with whom I have worked have found the most meaningful. You should use whatever scores give you the most accurate, useful information. Some research workers have found it makes little difference to score the choice and, therefore, count each choice as one.

While there are many ways of presenting the group's nominations in a picture, the ones illustrated in Figure 9 and Figure 11 are the ones my colleagues and I have found to be most efficient—shortest time to construct and most information provided. Figure 11 is usually constructed on 8½″ x 11″ paper which has been divided into four concentric circles. Each circle in the sociogram represents a fourth of the members so the scores of the members are listed in order and divided into four groups. In our group of eight, two boys are in each fourth. If it were a group of twenty, five would be in each circle. The members are arranged with high scorers in the middle and with as few of the lines showing nominations crossing as is possible.

It may be useful in the sociogram to show specific factors related to member nomination by dividing it into halves or quarters. To highlight male-female factors in choices the men would be put in one half and the women in the other. In an agency planning committee it might be useful to show the relations of old members and new members as well as male-female. To do this the sociogram would be divided into quarters as illustrated in Figure 13.

Peer nominations and sociograms can be very exciting to look at and put social relations into a very alive, action-oriented context. To give them even greater reality and dynamics, photographs of the members' faces are pasted on the sociogram in place of the circles or triangles. In showing a sociogram to members or in using it with other staff, there is a tendency to assess "nearness to the center" as the more favored position and assume they are the more valuable or worthwhile members. This is not meant to be the purpose of a sociogram and, in fact, half-in and half-out members may provide the linking relationships which hold the group together. There is also a tendency for the creators of the sociogram to become over-enthusiastic about the tool and try to show too much in it. A sociogram that shows three choices for fifteen or more people becomes very

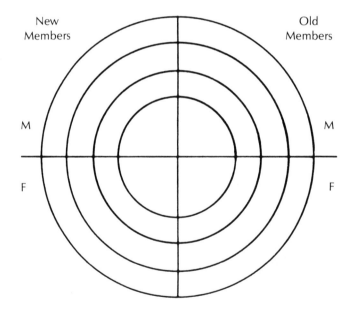

Division of a sociogram to show old members-new members and male-female relations.

Figure 13

complicated and turns people off. For this reason I have found a combination of weighted scores and presentation of only first choices (perhaps two choices in smaller groups) as in Figure 11, to be the most all-around useful.

Presentation of Individual Relationships

Teachers, counselors, and group workers interested in exploring the unique relationships of individuals will want to look at a separate profile. This could be especially useful with high-influence members and problem or deviant members. A separate, individual profile for a high-influence member spotlights the people nominating him or her who are the members most likely to be influenced by him or her. The nominations of the problem member or deviant member indicate the people who hold some promise of serving as role models or standard setters. A separate chart for Grant Ruple in the Anzacks group looks like the one presented in Figure 14.

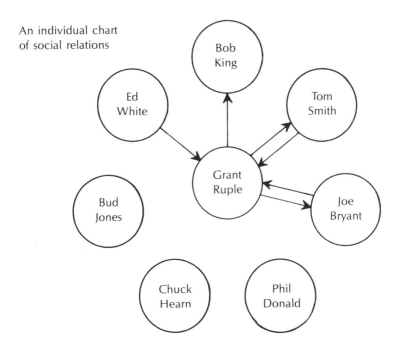

Figure 14

122 Groups: Leadership and Group Development

Reciprocal Friendships

The method of establishing acceptance scores for each member was illustrated in Figures 10 and 11, and another score for reciprocal friendships adds additional information. Some members may be well accepted by other members in a group, yet upon analysis of their own choices it is found that they do not choose the members who have chosen them. A reciprocal friendship is one in which two members have chosen each other and are identified on the sociogram as a pair (see Figure 15). If a person makes three choices it is possible that all three of those chosen may choose him or her in return. If this is the case the reciprocal friendship score is three. If only two of those chosen chose him or her in return, the score would be two.

First choice = 5
Second choice = 3
Third choice = 2

Worker _____ Scudder _____
Group _____ Anzacks _____
Date _____ May 2nd _____

RECIPROCAL FRIENDSHIP CHART
(In-group choices)

LAST NAMES	Chosen							
	1. Grant Ruple	2. Bob King	3. Tom Smith	4. Joe Bryant	5. Phil Donald	6. Chuck Hearn	7. Bud Jones	8. Ed White
1. Ruple		5	(3)	(2)				
2. King			(3)		(5)			(2)
3. Smith	(5)	(3)				(2)		
4. Bryant	(2)	5						(3)
5. Donald		(5)				(3)	(2)	
6. Hearn				(3)				5
7. Jones			(2)		(3)	5		
8. White	3	(5)		(2)				
TOTALS	10	23	8	4	11	8	4	10

Reciprocal friendships in the Anzacks group

Figure 15

A Group Cohesion Index

One of the best indicators of a group's cohesion is based on the percentage of reciprocal friendships. The formula of group cohesion is the number of mutual friendships divided by the possible number of pairs in the group. Let us take the case of the Anzacks as an example. In looking at Figure 15 we see that there are nine reciprocal friendships in the group. To establish the total number of mutual friendships possible we multiply the maximum number of choices per person—in this case three—by the total number of the group minus one and divide by two.

$$\text{Cohesion} = \frac{\text{Number of mutual friendships}}{\text{Number of possible mutual friendships}} = \frac{9}{3\,(N - 1) \div 2}$$

$$\text{Cohesion} = \frac{9}{3\,(8 - 1) \div 2} = \frac{9}{3\,(7) \div 2} = \frac{9}{21 \div 2} = \frac{9}{10.5} = .857$$

$$\text{Cohesion} = .857$$

The cohesion score of .857 for the Anzacks is very high, as the scores would range from zero to one. If this score were expressed in percent you might say it was an 86 percent cohesive group.

An even more meaningful indicator of group cohesion is prepared by allowing members to nominate people who are both in and outside the group—nominations are not restricted to group members—and then determining the percent of group members chosen. Part 1 described that a group's cohesion was clearly related to the members' attraction to the group. Attraction to a group will be higher where members like and respect the other participants. Thus, if we ask the members of a hockey team to list their ten best friends and eight of Chris' choices are on the team, we would expect her to be more attracted to the team than Dale, who only nominated three other team members. Low attraction scores help to explain absences, lack of enthusiasm for group activities, nonconformity to group standards, and possible interpersonal difficulties with other members.

A group attraction or cohesion index for the total group can be made by averaging the attraction scores of all the members. Not limiting nominations to group members makes the information more realistic and lifelike. The questions can vary with the type of group.

Social Agency Board. List the ten people in this city whose opinion it would be most important for you to hear on a social problem concerning local people.

High School Class. List the five youths of your age group that you spend the most time with after school and on weekends.

Any Group. If we were putting together a steering committee to revitalize our group (team, department, unit, or whatever), who would be the most important people to have on it? List the names of the five you would choose below.

It has been my experience that such a group attraction index is a very real measure of group cohesion and serves well as a check on cohesion estimated through the group observation procedures described in Part 2. Our rule of thumb in evaluating group growth is to have three different measures of the group dimension being assessed. In the case of cohesion we have observation and a sociometric attraction index as two; the third could be an estimation by the group members themselves. Repeating the same three measures over a period of time would give quite an accurate picture of the group's health related to that dimension.

THE SOCIAL RELATIONS SCALE

Another method of establishing the social acceptance of members in a group allows a member to rate his liking for every other member of the group. Each member of the group rates the other group members on a five-point scale as in Figure 16. The social relations score (see Figure 17) of an individual is calculated by counting the number of times others described him in the first column (would like to have him/her as one of my best friends) and multiplying it by five, then doing the same for all the checks in the second column and multiplying by four, on down to the last column and multiplying by one. This score is then divided by the number of people rating him (total number of the group minus one) and the results may range from a low of one to a high of five. How well an individual accepts others in the group can be calculated by summing the score of the ratings he or she made of other members in the group and again dividing by the number of choices made.

The social relations scale has the advantage over a sociometric measure based on three to five choices in that each member can repeat a feeling about every other member. This may indicate that all members feel

| Group | Anzacks | Name | Grant Ruple |
| Worker | Scudder | Date | March 6th |

Social Relations Check Sheet

Below are listed the other members of the group. Every one has different ideas about those with whom they work and play. Check one of the spaces on the right to tell how you feel about your group's members.

GROUP MEMBERS	Very glad to have him/her in the group and want him/her as one of my best friends.	Would like to have him/her in my group but not as a close frend.	Would like to be with him/her once in a while but not too much.	Don't mind him/her being in our group but don't want much to do with him/her.	I would not choose him/her to be in our group.
Bob King	×				
Tom Smith	×				
Joe Bryant	×				
Phil Donald		×			
Chuck Hearn		×			
Bud Jones		×			
Ed White	×				

Grant rates the other members of his group for the Social Relations Scale.

Figure 16

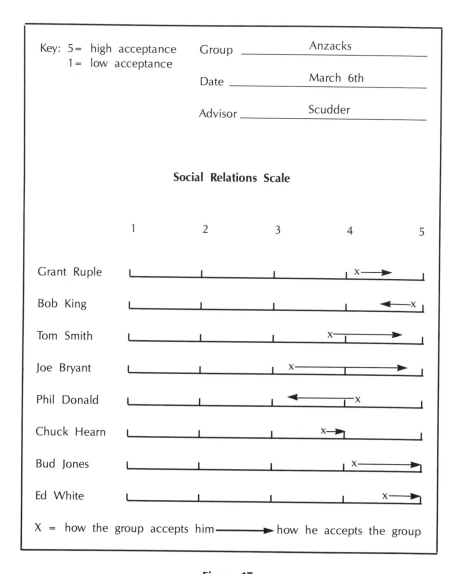

Figure 17

very positive about one another, which would not be as clear from a limited choice sociogram. In this way it compares favorably with an open sociogram (not restricted to group members).

The major disadvantage of a social relations index is that it can be less discriminating (all the members can be lumped in the same box), and the possibility of members being rated as "not chosen to be in the group" may be more difficult to talk about than simply not being chosen in a forced-choice sociogram. The reader may check to see which tells the most about a group by comparing Figure 11 with Figure 16.

Member Ratings

The term "member ratings" is used to differentiate ratings based on non-friendship criteria from friendship choices. Research has shown that ratings of group members by other group members are often more accurate in identifying character and leadership qualities than other measures and they are more practical to carry out. And, member ratings with their high consistency give a rather true picture of the member being rated. The areas in which people can be rated by others who know them are very broad, but of most interest to human service workers are the areas related to their programs. Thus, ratings usually focus on personality, skills, and likely

---

Peer Rating

Fill in each space with the name of the person in that group that fits there best.

1. During the meeting, I agree most with what _____ said.

2. Of everyone, _____ seemed to get the most out of the meeting.

3. _____ and I seemed to understand each other pretty well.

4. I felt the group didn't treat _____ very fairly.

5. I couldn't agree much with what was said by _____.

6. _____ helped the group along the most today.

7. It seemed that _____ was not included by the group.

8. _____ and _____ competed most for leadership.

A. Who is learning the most in this program? _____

B. Who always has lots of ideas of things to do? _____

C. Who enjoys the program most? _____

D. Who would you choose as chairperson? _____

Peer Rating

Check off the items that apply to the person you are describing.

_____ Gave support to individual members

_____ Made proposals about what the group should do

_____ Reduced conflict between individual members

_____ Withdrew from the group's activity

_____ Relieved group tension with a joke or comment

_____ Tried to dominate and control the group

---

behavior of program participants. Or, they ask about changes in behavior that may be related to participating in the program under study. For example, training programs often ask participants in the program who they think increased their skills or understanding most in the program. Co-workers or people living with the program participants may also be asked to rate them in the relevant areas of skill development. Friends of participants in a training program for disadvantaged youth were asked to assess changes in participants' morale, and parents of youth in a diabetic camp were asked to assess any changes in their child's taking responsibility for the treatment of his or her physical condition, such as self-administration of insulin. Other peer nominations ask for the names of the five people most likely to be able to get a new project off the ground in this community (or school, church, social agency).

Member ratings may focus on a specific area of interest to the group and ask for "the three people most likely to use the learning from this program in their daily life" or "who are the three people in the unit most likely to do agency work on their own time?" Another variation lists a number of things people might do (volunteer to work on a project, visit a sick member at home) and asks members to put in the names of anyone in the group who would do these things. For children under twelve, the list of things people might do can take on a "guess-who" format. "Here is someone who would share candy with another group member—guess who." The members are then asked to list the names of those in the group, including themselves, who fit the description.

Another way of handling peer nominations or descriptions is to have all the members rank themselves and all the other members for each item on the list of things people might do. This approach is most appropriate in a small group (less than fifteen) where the members know each other fairly well. In response to a question of "careful listening" everyone ranks each other and themselves from most to least. This gives a rather complete and accurate picture of how members see each other. Checking a member's self-ranking against the average of those given by other members shows the accuracy of that person's self-perception. For an example of this procedure let's consider its use with the tool "Roles of Group Members" (page 96) by a college student executive board. The eleven members of the student board ranked each other on each of the roles described in this tool from who takes this role most often to who performs it least often. The results were tabulated by a volunteer following the format of Figure 18 and returned to each member. The results showed the members the roles others saw them performing most and least frequently compared to the others. And, it showed how accurately they perceived their roles in the group.

Task Roles	High								Low		
							Name Bluma Hackett				
Defines problems	11	1	1	S1	1	111		1			
Seeks information		1	11		1	S	1	11		1	1
Gives information	1		1		S	111	111	1	1		
Seeks opinions	1	11	11	111		1		S			
Gives opinions	1	1111	111	S							
Tests feasibility	111	11	111	S	1				1		

Member rankings of an individual on task roles performed in the group. The solid line shows the average group ranking while the broken line is the self-ranking. Each mark "1" represents the ranking by a group member and the "S" is the self-ranking.

Figure 18

Figure 18 shows a partial summary (task roles only) of a member of the executive board. It shows that Bluma has a rather accurate picture of herself as a just-above-average member in performing task roles but underestimates her "opinion-seeking" role.

Although the results were returned to the members for their personal use, the group discussed general interpretations. At the next two meetings they practiced the roles they wanted to improve and discussed the results at the end of the meeting.

In summary, member ratings give information that is descriptive of an individual and may provide an indication of reputation or social status. They do not, compared to sociograms, give much sense of a group's social system or interaction patterns.

Other Uses of Sociometric Choices

Often a group cannot be understood by itself and must be studied in relation to the other groups and people in its environment. The sociometric idea can be easily extended to show the relationship between two groups, or among several groups. Intergroup sociograms may be constructed along the lines of Figure 13 or some similar method which separates the groups. It can also be useful to extend the sociometric technique and show the relationship and relative status of groups as if they were individuals. Thus, individuals would be asked to nominate other groups or units instead of individuals.

Part 1 talked about the value of groups having a well-defined hierarchy where all participants know what is expected of them and what they can expect from each other. Accuracy in perceiving the status and roles of group participants increases the effectiveness of the worker and the members, especially those in key positions. Sociograms clearly showing status hierarchies are constructed from questions such as "List in order the five people in this group to whom you most frequently look for leadership" or "Which five members of this group usually determine what is going to happen? List them in order of influence."

In summary it can be said that those people working with groups usually have a pretty good idea from their systematic observations of the interpersonal relationships in their group. Typically, these observation hunches are about 60 percent accurate with considerable room left for the data provided by a sociogram to improve the accuracy of these observations. When I use a sociometric measurement, I write down my predictions of what the results will be and over the years I have found this one of the best professional development experiences to sharpen up my observational skills and accent my biases. Sociograms show the important interpersonal dynamics in a group and when used at two or more points in time, highlight the growth or changes within the group. Above all, sociograms provide the framework for understanding the group behavior of members that may otherwise seem unexplainable.

OTHER DATA COLLECTION METHODS

Program Locators and Interest Finders

One of the most frequently used tools to gather information about a group is some kind of interest survey. It may be called a needs analysis, an interest census, or a program locator as it identifies programs or activities that are desired by the members. The survey may take the form of a check-off sheet with a list of interests or activities, and participants are asked to check those that are of interest and double check the most important items. Members may also be asked to list or to check off the expectations they have for the group. Such a list might include:

- Make new friends
- Improve physical fitness
- Feel better about myself

Interest Survey
(Girl Scouts, abridged)

Read each activity and put a check mark (✔) beside the ones you have done sometime in the past year. Put a line under those you'd like to do.

_____ Helping the troop produce a play	_____ Organizing a patrol as a patrol leader
_____ Making a sculpture with wood or clay	_____ Learning about physical fitness
_____ Setting up a weather station at a campout	_____ Organizing a bicycle safety course
_____ Making a model of the solar system	_____ Learning about black music
_____ Helping to plan activities for the troop	_____ Learning how to patent an invention

---

- Work on a service project
- Learn new skills
- Travel to different places

Such surveys provide a clear picture of what a group wants to do together and general expectations for their membership. This information is valuable in understanding why members are in the group, what is motivating them, and what will help them become more involved. Redoing a needs analysis at a second point in time provides valuable data to estimate group growth through comparisons.

Interest groups are also a rich source of data about the individuals who compose a group. They can be used to tell if a person:

1. Has interests more or less mature than his or her age group; or typical interests when gender, geographical location, education, and ethnic and religious affiliation are considered.
2. Has preferences for kinds of activity, such as hard-soft, spectator-active, structured-creative, self-directed-leader-led, individual-group, competitive-cooperative, and so forth.
3. Has interests congruent to those of the program or values similar to those of the agency. The extent to which interests and values become more congruent measures the impact of program participation.

The most useful interest surveys are "home grown" to fit a specific group and situation and the above examples should help you to make up your own. Charting the changing interests of individuals, groups, and staff teams is a powerful method of assessing the effectiveness of human service programs.

Attitude and Personality Surveys

There are hundreds of attitude and personality surveys available for all purposes.[13] They represent a broad range of areas and it is usually easier to use one that has been carefully prepared and its usefulness established than to make up one of your own.

---

[13]Dale Lake and others, *Measuring Human Behavior.* New York: Teachers College, Columbia University, 1973. John Robinson and Paul Shaver, *Measures of Social Psychological Attitudes.* Ann Arbor, MI: Institute for Social Research, University of Michigan, 1973. Marvin Shaw and Jack Wright, *Scales for the Measurement of Attitudes.* New York: McGraw-Hill, 1967.

The Dimock Leadership Inventory[14] was designed to assess attitudes toward leadership along a directive-participative continuum and to measure personality traits of flexibility, open-mindedness, and interdependence. It has been used with a fair amount of success in understanding the behavior of individuals in groups, identifying high-success leaders, and evaluating training programs for group leaders, street workers, and nursing and recreation personnel. Samples from it are shown below.

DIMOCK LEADERSHIP INVENTORY

1. You would like to tell certain people a thing or two.

2. When a group is undecided about what to do, the leader should solve the problem by making the decision for the group.

34. If people would talk less and work more, everyone would be better off.

23. It is up to the leader to put a member in his or her place when his or her behavior is upsetting the group.

Typical areas of focus of the available inventories and surveys include:
- Moral judgment and values
- Locus of control
- Personal rigidity
- Trust and acceptance of others
- Socio-political attitudes
- Various personality traits
- Social issues and problems
- Use of coping behaviors
- Sexual behavior
- Self-esteem
- Alienation
- Attitudes toward authority

---

[14]Hedley G. Dimock, *The Dimock Leadership Inventory*. Orange, CA: Sheridan Psychological Services, 1969.

- Social sensitivity
- Religious attitudes
- Family relations
- Ethnic and religious groups
- Styles of leadership
- Interest inventories

Personal Data from Members

Many agencies routinely collect basic personal information when starting work with a new program participant. This "face sheet" type of information usually includes name, age, sex, address and telephone number, marital status, education, place of employment, and so on. While some of these personal areas have recently been forbidden through human rights legislation, many organizations continue to record extensive information about their clients. In some organizations (health units, colleges, social services, and special needs programs), this information is supplemented with either an intake interview or an extensive written questionnaire. It may also include a needs assessment (what are the present problems that need help) or in the case of a college, summer camp, or recreation department, an interest survey asking how the participant wants to use the resources available. These records are often overlooked as a very rich source of information that can help to understand participants and plan for the full utilization of their skills and resources. They also form a baseline profile useful in evaluating group growth.

Autobiographies and diaries are also a useful and sometimes readily available source of information for understanding individual members and analyzing groups. Many educational and training programs require an autobiography for admission. In some of the group research I have designed we have asked participants to write a very brief one- or two-page autobiographical statement about themselves, their families, friends, and interests. We were overwhelmed with the quality and depth of information presented. In the human services we don't want to spend our time collecting tons of data we won't use; hence, our rule of thumb is keep the statement very short and increase its relevance by asking a few leading questions such as the ones above.

A more easily used form is an autobiographical episode report form such as "What is the most important part of your life right now?", "Talk a bit about the most important experience in your life," or "Describe the people in your life that you have admired the most."

During the teens, boys and especially girls keep diaries of their activities, thoughts, and personal reactions to people and situations. College and university students may keep learning logs. Adults keep appointment calendars. Program participants may share the records they have or start keeping specific information if they are sure the information will be useful to their group or future programs.

Other self-reports take the form of asking members to describe "their three wishes" or "What would you like to be doing three years from now?". Youth may be asked to describe "what I did last summer" or "the person in my life I admire the most." There are also a number of commercial self-report inventories on the market such as the Bell Adjustment Inventory and the Mooney Problem Check List—see footnote 13 for more information on them.

Member Reports on Programs

Member reactions to group situations and activities are just as accurate and useful a source of information as the member reactions and ratings of each other described in the earlier part of this section. This useful source of data is often overlooked in the belief that the members don't know very much about what is really going on in the group. However, member reactions usually give a more reliable and often a truer picture of the group's situation than does an evaluation by the worker. Probably the most natural way for members to supply information on their reactions to the group is through a descriptive, narrative writing or diary. Very often a group has a secretary whose job it is to write up a record of the meeting. This may supply some information but it is usually not personal enough—doesn't tell how the writer felt or how the others seemed to feel—to give a comprehensive picture. In order to provide more than a factual account of a meeting or group activity, a group can use two people to prepare records. One tells what happened, what decisions or plans were made, and is a *content* record (perhaps kept by the secretary or group recorder). The other is a *process* report and tells how things happened, giving hunches about how members felt in connection with observations of their individual behavior. This is a personal report more in the stance of a group observer.

Many of the observation tools described in Part 2 can be used by group members to give focus to their reactions and reports on programs. *The Survey of Group Development* was designed for this kind of use as it gives an overview of a group on the major dimensions of group growth. Figure 19 shows the composite ratings of a young adult group by its members, its workers, and the agency program supervisor on the *Survey of Group Development*.

Survey of Group Development

Member's rating _____ Worker's rating _ _ _ _ _ _ _ Supervisor's rating . . . .

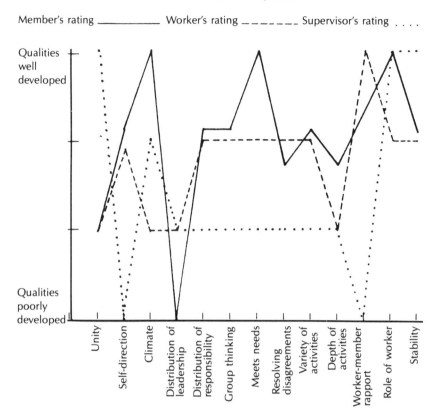

Member ratings of the group are summarized and compared to ratings by the group worker and agency program supervisor.

Figure 19

It is particularly worthwhile to take some time toward the end of a meeting or activity and ask members either verbally or in writing to give their reactions. The "end-of-meeting reports" and "post-meeting reaction forms" (PMR's) can help focus these reactions and by comparing the results from session to session, progress can be assessed. Members can also be asked to discuss or report on such basic questions as: problems we had in our group today; how the group could have improved its effectiveness; important things that happened that everyone may not have noticed; how I felt in the group today.

In my experience workers report a very strong commitment to doing some kind of a post-meeting evaluation but continually report that the session ran overtime and there was no time to do the PMR they had planned. To deal with this common concern (and I have also experienced it frequently), we developed a contingency PMR. The one-minute PMR is shown below. The five-minute version of it with immediate feedback to any size group up to 100 has the facilitator putting the two scales on newsprint, chalkboard, or overhead projector and explaining their meaning. All participants are then asked to identify a point on the scale that represents their assessment and raise their hands when that point is called out. The facilitator quickly counts the hands in response to the calling out of the numbers from one to five, records the number responding to each number on the chart, and makes a quick calculation of the average on each scale to sum up the meeting. This is a big winner for which there is always time.

Post-Meeting Reaction
(One minute)

1. How well did we do today in accomplishing our task? (Circle the point on the scale that most nearly represents your opinion.)

   TASK ACCOMPLISHMENT

1	2	3	4	5
poor	fair	satisfactory	good	excellent

2. How well did we do today in working as a group and building our relationships?

   GROUP BUILDING

1	2	3	4	5
poor	fair	satisfactory	good	excellent

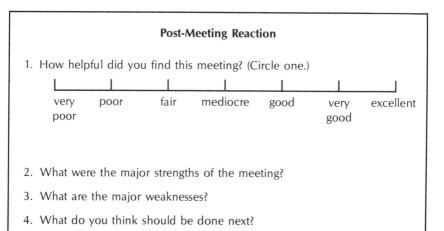

Post-Meeting Reaction

1. How helpful did you find this meeting? (Circle one.)

very   poor   fair   mediocre   good   very   excellent
poor   good

2. What were the major strengths of the meeting?

3. What are the major weaknesses?

4. What do you think should be done next?

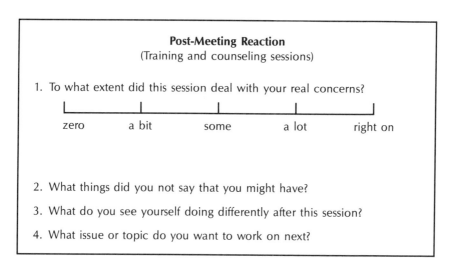

Post-Meeting Reaction
(Training and counseling sessions)

1. To what extent did this session deal with your real concerns?

zero   a bit   some   a lot   right on

2. What things did you not say that you might have?

3. What do you see yourself doing differently after this session?

4. What issue or topic do you want to work on next?

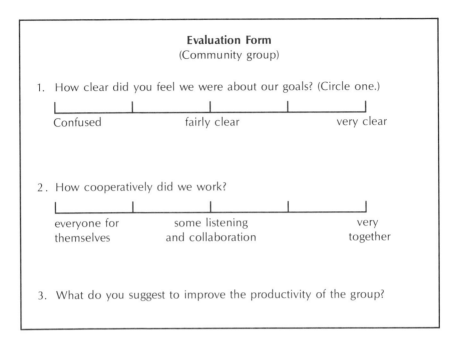

Reports from Others

Useful information about a group or about its members can be collected from people close to the group or its members. They may be participants in other programs in the agency with whom this group interacts or they may be "significant others" of the members such as spouses, special friends, parents, siblings, or work colleagues. Students in a school usually have very clear pictures of what they think of the other classes they are not taking and those "others" living with a program member are astute observers of changes in behavior, attitudes, or skills of that member as they surface in the daily living setting. To be sure, these others provide an excellent second opinion about any group analysis the group or its worker is making.

Chapter 8

Measuring Individual and Group Growth

Thorndike once said that anything that exists, exists in some amount and that amount can be measured. Human behavior has been very difficult to measure, yet in recent years the behavioral sciences have made great advances in assessing both individual and group growth.

Many group programs are like a merry-go-round. There is action, excitement, and fun, but the participants get off right where they got on. There has been a lot of activity but everyone ends up just where they started. To prevent programs from becoming merry-go-rounds, there needs to be clearly stated, measurable goals and regular assessment of movement toward these goals. It is this process that separates educational and recreational programs from those that are just occupying people's time.

The rapidly increasing percentage of all money that is spent on human service programs—education, social welfare, recreation, and health services—has accelerated the expectation that these programs would provide some objective evidence of the usefulness of their work. Usually there is a direct relationship between the quality of a human service program and its efforts to systematically assess the impact of its work in relation to its stated goals.

The most important function of group appraisal is to help the group and the worker understand the factors affecting their efforts to improve the group's operation. Many of the observation guides, sociometric devices, and rating scales described in Part 2 and in Chapter 7 can be used with little additional effort to measure group growth. A measurement design may do nothing more than plan to use the information collected from the regular use of these tools in a comparative way to show changes within the group. The methods and procedures described here to measure individual and group growth can be used by staff who have not had research and statistical training.

RELIABILITY, VALIDITY, AND STATISTICAL SIGNIFICANCE

These terms, frequently used in measurement, are useful ones for the group worker to understand. The term *reliability* refers to the degree that a repeated measure by the same procedure gives similar results. For example, a twelve-inch ruler is usually very reliable as a tool to measure the width of a desk. A piece of string would be a much less reliable measuring tool for the same purpose as it is subject to stretching. A reliable measuring tool should also be accurate and precise. Suppose you wanted to find the length of time it takes sound to travel one mile. If you made several tests and timed each one with a stopwatch, calibrated in fractions of seconds, you would be much more likely to get the same answer than if you used a regular wristwatch. Both watches are reliable but the stopwatch is more precise to start and stop and can be read more accurately. Before we can measure anything we must have reasonably reliable measurement tools.

The term *validity* refers to the extent a measurement produces relevant information about the subject being measured. Does the test or tool measure what we want it to measure? This is the question raised in seeking validity. The more valid an instrument is, the more it is able to predict what it is we want to know about. A ruler is considered a very valid tool for linear measurement as it will predict whether our desk will fit through a given doorway.

Statistical significance tells the likelihood of there being a real, non-chance change between two measurements. Change within a group over a period of time may be due to chance changes or normal fluctuations within the group. A test of statistical significance is needed to determine the likelihood that the change is not due to these factors. A study of the weight of ten boys may show an average gain of half a pound in two weeks. A test of significance gives the worker an indication of whether this was due to chance changes and inaccuracies in measurement or whether it indicated an actual weight gain on the part of the boys.

While the terms reliability, validity, and statistical significance are in constant use in almost all of the program evaluation reports, they do not meet our needs. We are interested in improving the programs we lead and in helping our organization establish priorities among its various programs in relation to their achievement of organization goals. First and foremost we want assessment information that we and our groups can use to increase our effectiveness. Hopefully, it will also help our agency to determine our contribution to what they are trying to do. Hence, our first criteria is *utilization*. Secondly, we want information about group growth that is *credible*, that people can believe is a true representation of the group. Group assessments are likely to be more accurate if they are *confirmable* and our rule of thumb is to try to triangulate important aspects of our measurements by looking at the same aspect from three different viewpoints. For example, indicators of a group's cohesion could come from observations, sociograms, and group records. Or, if the most practical source of the data is from observations, then they should come from three different people with different perspectives, such as a member, the group worker, another agency staff member, or a visitor. These three criteria fit together and build on each other, for the more confirmable the measurements are, the more likely they will be seen as credible and trustworthy, and the more trust and confidence people have in the data, the more likely they are to use it in group planning.

WHAT CAN BE EVALUATED

In general, there are three kinds of things that can be measured in a program to analyze and evaluate individual and group growth.

1. Changes in behavior, life style, or well-being of individual members in their daily lives.
2. Changes in knowledge, sensitivity, attitudes, self-understanding, and skills of members as they relate to program goals.
3. Changes in the group dimensions related to growth, such as climate, involvement, interaction, cohesion, and productivity. This could be extended to include evaluations of group composition, content, leadership, and activities in relation to the stated goals and objectives for the group.

Agency goals often expect their programs will change the behavior of participants in their daily life, yet in practice, staff rarely evaluate it. Participants may report in some kind of a program follow-up what they think they are doing differently. Or, their co-workers, family, and friends may be asked to describe the changes they have noted which may be related to participating in the agency's program. This area is usually given to outside researchers/evaluators if it is studied and has little to do with day-to-day program planning.

Most human service evaluation looks at changes in participants' knowledge, attitudes, and skills, or at changes in group dimensions and related program information. Technical skills, such as physical strength and endurance, or artistic, musical, or mechanical skills are a focus of evaluation activities. This is the usual approach to school subjects. Our culture shows a keen interest in what people know and what they can do.

OTHER MEASURES OF GROUP AND AGENCY GOALS

Membership figures and other indirect appraisals are frequently used to evaluate group programs. Some indirect measures are fairly useful while others are quite doubtful. Figures of the gross number of people served or yearly attendance records tell very little. They may show an increase from one year to the next and this suggests that the agency is popular. Any large movie theater could probably report larger attendance and by the same token should be considered more popular. If the attendance figures are used to imply effectiveness in servicing the community, the theater would have to be given credit for doing a "better job." Attendance figures that are broken down to show the number of hours per month members spent in agency programs and the turnover of members has more meaning. A further breakdown into age groups shows if the agency is working with the groups its goals and policies imply.

Membership statistics, attendance in different programs, and program content give information about agency organization, but tell nothing about the achievement of specific goals. The number of members in large and small groups with a ratio of staff or advisors to these groups is more important for there is evidence to show that personal growth and specific skills, such as swimming, are best achieved in small groups. Small groups with appropriate leadership are important, but this in itself does not mean that members are growing and developing, only that there is a greater possibility of them doing so.

An analysis of program content shows if there is a logical connection between the program and the agency goals. An agency with physical education goals builds its program around the learning and practice of a variety of physical skills and the practice of good health habits. An informal education agency builds its program around group experiences where new behavior and values can be learned, discussed, and practiced in the program. A review of program content and the percentage of members participating in different activities helps an agency check the degree to which its program is planned with agency objectives in mind.

Part 1 described research studies which showed a relationship between the workers' personality and style of leadership and the behavior and growth of members in their group. The research suggested that participative, group-centered leaders were more likely than dominating, directive leaders to have healthy groups and positive member growth. The study of these aspects of leadership has been a popular indirect measure of goal achievement potential in different situations. The Dimock Leadership Inventory is an example of a short questionnaire that can be used for this purpose with considerable validity and credibility.

UTILIZATION-FOCUSED ASSESSMENTS

The assessments made of individual and group growth have as their purpose the improvement of the effectiveness of the group. Thus, a useful appraisal clarifies areas where improvements can be made. Occasionally, an evaluation of two or more programs will help a worker or an agency establish where time and money are best spent, but most of the time the focus is on improving the program. Especially important in these attempts to analyze and evaluate group growth are tentative answers to the questions that will guide the workers' intervention and organization planning (size of group, length and frequency of meetings, program focus, communication with other groups, etc.).

From our many years of experience in helping hundreds of human service agencies, a few principles have emerged for increasing the likelihood that appraisal activities will help the group become more effective.

1. Whatever is done should be done on a more or less ongoing basis.
2. Everyone should know what is going to happen and, if appropriate, be involved in the assessment activity (observing, doing peer nominations, keeping records, collating and analyzing data, or wherever they can help). The greater the group's involvement, the greater the probability of the assessment leading to action planning and implementation.
3. Keep the assessments simple and easy to manage.
4. Quality, not quantity, is the goal. Piaget, the world-famous French psychologist, rarely studied more than ten children in any project.
5. Select critical incidents, situations, or individuals for more in-depth study.
6. Try to have multiple perspectives (triangulation) for all important areas.

Time and again in our evaluation activities we have found that if people are presented with very credible data by a group worker (and especially an outsider), they were not likely to make use of it even if the implications were clear and related to the group's concerns. But, if the same information was collected by the group members, it was put to use. Out of these experiences came our new approach to increasing the effectiveness of groups and organizations called Systems Improvement Research,[15] grounded on the principle of member participation in the assessment and improvement of activities.

ASSESSMENT DESIGNS

To appraise the results of a program there needs to be a design or plan to collect relevant information, a selection of the methods and tools to collect the information, and some method of analyzing and interpreting the information. Let's turn now to the first of these considerations.

The purpose of the assessments described here is to improve the effectiveness of the group. To do this, the group, and more especially the staff worker, needs to understand what is happening in the group and why it is happening. There is a need to know the basis of program successes and how they can be built on and made even more successful. Program criteria is always in terms of strengths and weaknesses, and not judgments such as fair, good, or excellent.

The Preferred Design

The single best design for collecting this relevant information is on an ongoing, regular basis. Collecting and perhaps analyzing the data are part of the regular activities of the group. This design is called a *"time-lapse design"*, which means that the data collection takes place at regular time intervals. This is the normal practice in many groups where attendance is taken at each session and there is some record or "minutes" of the meeting. The recruitment of new members takes place at regular times and is followed with orientation and indoctrination activities. The one addition that would be new for many groups in using a time-lapse design is including a follow-up measurement or questionnaire after the group's program is over or a member has withdrawn. The addition of a follow-up measurement shortly after the program has concluded or several members have left identifies the permanency of any change resulting from the program.

---

[15]H. Dimock, *Intervention and Collaborative Change.* Guelph, Ontario: University of Guelph, 1981.

The *"after-only design"* is very familiar to us as most of our educational experiences included a final exam in school and a program evaluation in informal educational programs. While these end-of-program evaluations are quite easy to do, they don't provide a lot of information about the program. As they aren't done until the end of the program, they can't be used to improve that program.

Before and After Designs

The most useful designs for program evaluation are extensions of good program planning procedures. Most community recreation programs are built around the assessed needs and interests of community participants and a practical evaluation design would see repeating the assessment at a later point in time and checking on how well the needs were being met. The beginning of a school year often includes establishing the reading and math level of the students to assist the teacher in planning appropriate-level work. These tests can be repeated halfway through the year to determine what progress has been made. Most counseling programs commence with the taking of a case history which lists the client's symptoms, problems, and major worries. Repeating the case history by way of updating any changes at a later point in time can highlight progress by comparing the symptoms, problems, and worries. The place to start your planning is with what you are presently doing with your programs and consider doing some of your data collection twice. This will give you material that you can compare to assess the impact of the program.

Control Group Designs

Everyone who watches television is familiar with the Crest toothpaste ads describing the differences in tooth decay between the experimental group (Crest) and the control group (brand X), and you may be wondering why this design hasn't been mentioned. Well, it's still the ideal design but a lot has happened in fifteen years. First, everyone knows about brand X and doesn't want to have anything to do with it. And, most workers in the human service area are increasingly concerned about human rights and feel it's unethical or inappropriate to leave people out of a service they want or need—and especially to pretend that they are getting it. Second, it isn't necessary to have a control group who receive "no treatment" to accurately evaluate a program. And third, a lot of progress has been made during these years in refining evaluation tools and methods and in understanding what really helps to improve programs—this has made control groups both less popular and less necessary for program development.

To the extent that it is necessary to have a very rigorously controlled evaluation, a control group may still be used, but an equally useful design without the drawbacks mentioned above goes as follows: The program or group to be studied is identified ahead of time and the participants are measured *before* they enter the program. As they enter the program, they repeat the measurements and do them a third time at the end of the program. The difference between the first and second measurements serves as the "control group" for they did not participate in the program under study during that time. Then, the difference between the second and third measurements established what impact, if any, the program under study had on them. If this difference is greater than what took place between the first and second control measurements, then it can be assumed that the difference is likely related to participating in the program.

A few years ago, my colleagues and I were consulting with two high schools as they introduced leadership training and human relations courses for their students, one for credit and one noncredit. Both school boards wanted some pretty hard data about the effectiveness of these programs and we used the design of measuring the students likely to participate the same amount of time before the program started as they were in the program. The students who took the course for five months were measured five months before the course started, the first day of the course, and during the next to last week of the course (so the results could be reported to them during the last week). This gave us comparable data on the amount of growth taking place through regular school activities and that occurring during the period students were taking the new course. In both schools students continued to grow and develop, but in one school the change was similar to what had taken place in the previous length of time. An extra attraction of this design was that all the students were very interested in getting individual reports on their progress and this helped them to assess their own learning in comparison with other students.

METHODS OF COLLECTING INFORMATION

There are five ways of collecting data that can be used to evaluate the program. The selection of the most appropriate method depends on the importance of the assessment (time and energy people are prepared to put into it), and on what fits into usual program activities. Those who are doing the program appraisal should also select an approach that is comfortable for them and that interests them.

1. *Self-reports.* You can ask the people (participants and workers) about themselves and their experiences.

2. *Reports from others.* You can ask others who know the participants about them and their experiences.

3. *Direct observations.* You can observe the participants and workers and general functioning of the organization.

4. *Performance outcomes.* You can test the participants and workers; do clinical exams; collect physical, financial, employment data, etc.; or do situational tests of simulated life situations.

5. *Review program and operation records.* You can check budget allocations, program schedules, job assignments, policy-making records, and general unit and community records.

Written Information Tests

Tests of knowledge and understanding are used to ascertain how much of the program information members have picked up and assimilated. These tests are usual in many educational programs. Similar tests may be handled verbally rather than in writing.

Written Questionnaires or Surveys

1. *Measures of attitudes, beliefs, personal orientations, or interests.* The Dimock Leadership Inventory is typical of these tools as are the numerous surveys of values, temperament, and personality.[16]

2. *Post-meeting reactions.* Typical samples of these, which are shown in Chapter 7, ask participants to give reactions to a specific meeting or program session. While it is usually done as a written questionnaire, it can also be done verbally. In a large group I may put two or three rating scales on a chalkboard and ask participants to raise their hand when I call out the

---

[16]Dale Lake and others, *Measuring Human Behavior.* New York: Teachers College, Columbia University, 1973. John Robinson and Paul Shaver, *Measures of Social Psychological Attitudes.* Ann Arbor, MI: Institute for Social Research, University of Michigan, 1973.

point on the scale they choose. Or, if there is coffee after the program, three or four interviewers can move about asking the post-meeting questions and get a pretty good sampling of responses.

3. *Needs assessments and interest finders.* These surveys, also described with samples in Chapter 7, ask members to list their interests or concerns in various areas related to the program. Or, a comprehensive list of interests or concerns may be provided and members may be asked to check off the ones that apply.

Self-Reports

1. Personal information sheet.
2. Autobiographical sketches.
3. Diaries or learning logs.

Descriptions and Ratings of Members

These may be self-ratings or descriptions, or they may be completed by other members or staff. They may be extended to include friends, family, or co-workers. Rating scales, standardized case studies for comparative purposes, anecdotal records or behavior descriptions, and critical incidents may be used to give greater meaning to these descriptions.

Peer Nominations and Sociograms

Participants can be asked to nominate members to fill various categories, such as team leader, social convener, or "someone who gets things done." The use of sociometric choices and the social relations index which have been extensively described are popular choices in this category. They can be used to analyze the social structure of the group and establish levels of group cohesion and attraction to the group which can then be used as indicators of group growth.

Group Records

Records kept by the group recorder, minutes kept by a secretary, and the workers' records provide considerable information about attendance, how the group spent its time, and plans for the future. They may also highlight special accomplishments and levels of members' participation. The attendance record shows the stability of the group and notes who is absent with what frequency and the rate of turnover in the group.

Descriptions or Ratings of Group Operation

These descriptions can be made by the members or staff, or perhaps by visitors or independent observers. The Survey of Group Development and other rating forms are shown as illustrations in Part 2. Another example of use of the Survey of Group Development is included at the end of this chapter.

Projective Descriptions of the Group

Information is collected from these techniques by exposing the members to a general stimulus to which they may respond in different ways. Members may be asked, for example, to draw a picture of the group. People in residential programs can be asked to draw a picture of the organization (camp, residence, or institution). Old magazines can be given to members who are asked to make a collage of cut-out pictures representing the group or perhaps their role in the group. Members can also be asked to put on a skit depicting the group or role play recent critical situations. Creating songs, poems, or fables about the group are productive projective methods.

Systematic Observations

This is the most frequently used method of group appraisal as everyone is always observing what is going on. The only problem is to make the observation systematic and confirmable. Part 2 describes the procedures and observation guides to upgrade the quality of observations. Several years of perfecting group observations in the Systems Improvement Research project found that the use of two observers—one of whom was a member of the group and the other an outside independent observer—was the most favorable approach (the best data for the least amount of time).

Video Recordings

With the common ownership of videocassette recorders, most groups have access to equipment to video record their group sessions. Groups are often excited about this extension of the observation method as members may not have seen themselves in "the movies" before. While the novelty quickly wears off, the enthusiasm to watch and discuss a session is a powerful stimulant for an analysis and appraisal of a group's operation. The advantage of a video recording is the opportunity it provides members to observe themselves interacting within the group. The feedback received from this kind of self-analysis may be more usable and have more impact than feedback received from others. Video recordings are also particularly useful in documenting the life of a group over a period of time so that the group can review its progress by comparing the visual records.

Interviews

Individual and group interviews are another way of collecting the information described under written questionnaires or surveys; self-reports; descriptions, nominations, and sociometric choices; and descriptions or ratings of group operation. It has been my experience that interviewing is worth the additional time in situations where the interviewer wants to build a relationship with the respondent, such as a group leader or board chairperson interviewing a new group member; or, where part of or a whole group can be interviewed and the participants will learn as much useful information from each other as will the interviewer. The other situations where interviews have been found appropriate are in program follow-ups where not all respondents will take the time to complete a written questionnaire. Here an interview, and especially a telephone interview, makes it possible and cost effective to hear from all the participants.

Simulations and Role Playing

Case problems have been used to some extent where group members are given some information about a situation and asked how they would handle it. These cases may be presented in written form, in film or video, through a role play or demonstration, or by having the person involved in the situation verbally present it to the group. In our leadership training programs we use written case studies, films such as *Twelve Angry Men* and *Twelve O'Clock High,* and role plays of typical leadership dilemmas to see how their responses reflect their understanding of program concepts. We also use games made up of short case descriptions coupled with multiple-choice answers which give them immediate feedback on their applications of leadership theory. Such methods help us all to assess their progress in understanding and applying new leadership techniques.

Change in Related Systems

Some groups have as their goal the education or change of other groups or organizations (affirmative action programs, social change groups, and community education groups). Other groups, such as college student executives, or a Rotary Club, "Y," or scouts, have a goal of providing leadership or community service to their related systems. These outside but related groups or systems can provide considerable feedback about the impact and effectiveness of the group under study. For example, a college's Center for Innovative Student Activities received a wealth of information when they sent a questionnaire asking about the impact of their activities to related students, faculty, and administration on campus.

ANALYZING AND INTERPRETING INFORMATION

In order to analyze your data, it is helpful to organize it into some kind of a framework or summary form from which hunches and interpretations can be made. If you are not sure where to start, the "eyeballing" technique is most likely to be helpful.

The "Eyeballing" Technique or Graphic Displays

A good place to start in summarizing and focusing your data is to display it graphically in a chart, diagram, graph, or listing of major points on newsprint-sized sheets of paper. In preparing the sheets I use different colors of felt-tipped markers to show categories of my data.

My students have developed a group eyeballing technique where they bring in the data from their human service activities on newsprint sheets, put them on the wall, and invite their classmates and me to help analyze the information. As we look at the data we ask a lot of questions and look for relationships in what we see. First, we look for categories or classes: "Does age or sex make a difference in enjoyment of the program?" "Does length of participation in the program make a difference?" "Does group size seem important?" "Are there any similarities among participants who think they learned the most?" Often, these exploratory questioning surveys lead to identifying some possible themes. These themes which we consider as possible "rules of thumb" ask that we look for supporting evidence of the theme (or negative evidence) elsewhere in the data. The next steps in data analysis, if any seem justified, become much clearer.

Numerical Scoring and Percentages

Much information can be put into categories on the basis of similarity in some respect and the results counted or tabulated. For example, the frequency with which members of a group perform different role functions can be determined using Roles of Group Members in Part 2. A numerical scoring of the observations of the group observer showed the following results.

Industrial Management Club (N = 18)			
	First Meeting	Third Meeting	Fifth Meeting
Task Roles	81	74	68
Group Roles	12	16	24
Individual Roles	2	10	8
(Number of Roles of Each Type per 100 Interactions)			

An analysis of this information suggested that the group had been successful in increasing their group-building roles, but the individual roles had stayed about the same.

Other typical areas that can be counted included attendance; number of program hours; frequency of verbal participation; number of products or projects completed; types of activities engaged in; phone calls or interactions between meetings; turnout for special events; and turnover in the group showing seasonal fluctuations and differentiating males and females, age groups, length of membership and geographic location or work group affiliation.

Information can also be put into categories that have some relationship to one another and scores assigned to the categories. In the following example of the Survey of Group Development (Part 2), scores were assigned to each of the four possible choices to each question, reflecting a judgment of their desirability. A score of 1 was assigned to the answer seen as least desirable and 4 to the most desirable. The degree of desirability is not exactly comparable for each question and a score of 2 is not twice as desirable as a score of 1. The result is a rough overview that helps to show important trends and facilitate an analysis of the data.

Scoring is very popular as a data analysis method as it was such an important part of our school experience. Everything was given a score (even gym) and when we asked, "How did I do?" we came to expect a score such as 27 out of 30 for an answer. Most of the nomination and sociometric techniques described here can be scored as can many of the observation guides. While scores appear to be easily compared and contrasted, they tend to distort and oversimplify the data and, therefore, are often most useful when coupled with a qualitative analysis method, such as characteristic differences or ranking.

Content and Process Analysis

In qualitative analysis the themes, nature, and characteristics of the data are explored to gain insights that may have been lost through rough scoring or tabulations. In *content analysis* the descriptive data is divided into smaller parts or categories related to the goals of the group. Thus, the categories might be related to leadership styles, communication patterns, or factors contributing to group cohesion. The categories for analysis can also be created around perceived functional differences such as setting up major headings based on what camp counselors described in their daily logs. Major headings or categories found in the logs were descriptions of what the group did, comments on how the group liked the activity, reports of unique behavior of individual campers, and personal comments by the counselor.

Example

A sample of five out of thirty clubs of high school youth was selected and early in the program the worker of each completed a Survey of Group Development (Part 2). At the same time the professional staff who supervised the club program also completed a Survey of Group Development, acting as an independent observer. Eight months later the worker and supervisor again completed the survey independently. Scores of 1 to 4 were arbitrarily assigned the four categories for each question, based on a judgment of their desirability.

CLUB SCORES EARLY AND LATE IN PROGRAM YEAR

		Club A B* A*	Club B B A	Club C B A	Club D B A	Club E B A	Average B A
D I M E N S I O N S O F G R O U P	1	3 — 3	3 — 4	2 — 3	3 — 3	2 — 4	2.6 — 3.4
	2	2 — 3	3 — 3	2 — 3	2 — 4	2 — 4	2.2 — 3.4
	3	2 — 4	2 — 3	2 — 4	2 — 3	1 — 3	1.9 — 3.4
	4	1 — 3	3 — 3	2 — 3	2 — 4	2 — 4	2 — 3.4
	5	1 — 3	3 — 4	1 — 2	3 — 3	3 — 4	2.2 — 3.2
	6	2 — 2	2 — 3	2 — 4	3 — 4	2 — 3	2.2 — 3.2
	7	3 — 3	1 — 4	2 — 3	2 — 3	2 — 4	2 — 3.4
	8	2 — 3	2 — 2	3 — 4	2 — 4	2 — 3	2.2 — 3.2
G R O W T H	9	2 — 4	2 — 3	1 — 3	3 — 4	3 — 3	2.2 — 3.4
	10	1 — 3	3 — 3	2 — 4	4 — 4	2 — 4	2.2 — 3.6
	11	3 — 3	2 — 3	1 — 4	4 — 4	3 — 3	2.6 — 3.4
	12	3 — 4	3 — 3	2 — 3	3 — 4	3 — 3	2.8 — 3.4
	13	2 — 2	2 — 4	3 — 3	2 — 3	2 — 4	2.2 — 3.2
Average		2.1 — 3.1	2.4 — 3.2	2.0 — 3.3	2.7 — 3.6	2.2 — 3.5	

*B — Before; *A — After

Process analysis looks at "how the group worked" as contrasted to the "what the group did" focus of content analysis. Usually the two go hand-in-hand, as the group's goal achievement is related to both effective group work and task accomplishment. In our Systems Improvement Research studies we use a process-oriented method that describes the unfolding of a program as it moves forward, noting particularly critical events, collecting documents and experience reports, and systematically observing the impact of the program on the group members and other related systems.

Force-Field Analysis

A force-field analysis can be pictured as a giant tug-of-war with the factors contributing to something pulling in one direction and the restraining factors pulling in the opposite direction. A force field might ask, "What are the forces contributing to the group's cohesion?" and "What are the forces detracting from it?" Or, more simply, it might be listing the factors strengthening the group's effectiveness and those weakening it.

An extension of the force-field analysis is the *pro-con technique* where we make up a list of the successes and failures of our special events and then look for themes or characteristic differences between the two categories. This technique may also ask that we look at factors relating to a critical decision the group is about to make. When an increase in the size of a group is considered, relevant information could be divided into pros and cons to facilitate further analysis and aid in decision making.

Characteristic Differences

After drawing up a force-field analysis or two lists or groups of data in the pro-con technique, it is possible to start eyeballing the two lists, looking for factors which are characteristic of list A but not of group B and vice versa. These factors do not have to be true for every item on the list but are generally characteristic of that group as a whole and in ways that are different from the other group. After you have noted the characteristic differences for each group, look them over and see if there are any general principles which account for the differences between the two lists. For example, in looking at the two lists of successful and unsuccessful special events at camp, it was noted that successful events (a) were planned more than a week ahead of the event, (b) had campers' participation in planning, (c) had four or more different activities, and (d) took place in the evening. These characteristic differences helped to evaluate the programs and establish principles for planning more successful special events for the rest of the camp season.

As an evaluation method several people will look over the two lists or groups of data and seek out the characteristic differences. If the goal is to help make decisions or improve program planning, the people looking at the lists will likely be people involved in the decision making or staff involved in the program planning. However, if the goal is to establish an unbiased evaluation, then outside *judges* will be used to establish the characteristic differences or rank the items. These judges (usually three to five), should not know anything more than necessary about the evaluation project and should be presented with the two lists or groups of data and asked to find as many characteristic differences as possible between the two lists. Ideally, the judges should be people who are knowledgeable in the field and familiar with the criteria they are being asked to use in judging the lists.

The essence of the method of characteristic differences is to create two groups which will differ in some way and compare data from them. The two groups can be created in many different ways: boys versus girls, classroom A versus classroom B, rapidly healing versus slow-healing patients, successful versus unsuccessful programs, long-term versus short-term participants, high versus low achievers, youth whose parents participate in the program versus those whose parents don't participate, and top half versus bottom half.

This method can be used with all the various data collection procedures described here, but it is particularly useful with descriptive data such as that collected by essays, diaries, descriptive program records, behavior descriptions, anecdotal records, thumbnail descriptions, process observations, and self-reports or descriptions. It can, however, also be used with peer ratings, sociometric measurements, reputation ratings, community and organizational assessments (indicators of the quality of life), needs assessments, and post-meeting reactions. It is the most useful method for analyzing the characteristics of successful and unsuccessful programs and helping groups to build on the strengths in their program.

Ranking

Ranking is the process of arranging a set of data from high to low according to some criterion. We are thinking in ranks when we ascertain the status hierarchy in our group, put members in a continuum according to their contribution to task accomplishment, or make up a list of member interests from most important to least important. Using the method of ranking, a great deal of qualitative or descriptive information can be put into comparative order more easily and analyzed more fully than putting it into specific categories which may be artificial and not promote establishing relationships. And, if it becomes important to establish more reliable relationships, rank-order correlations are the most time effective to do.[17]

REPORTING BACK TO YOUR GROUP

Before you plan a report or make up a diagnostic analysis to present to the group, let me remind you that involvement in a group's analysis and diagnosing its strengths and weaknesses are more powerful motivators than receiving crisp, well-presented conclusions or a credible, well-documented report. Thus, I suggest that before you consider carrying the ball through the data analysis phase you consider ways of involving the group in analyzing and interpreting the data. In addition to increasing their interest in revitalizing their group, you'll gain their experience in the group to give additional perspective in analyzing the data. Data analysis and interpretation is usually done best as a group activity to optimize the group-building potential, and some kind of graphic or pictorial summary is helpful to work from as well as digests of the raw data. It may be productive to set aside a special meeting or at least part of a regular one for this group activity.

Another rule of thumb is to arrange these data analysis and interpretative sessions as soon after the data is collected as is practical. This was a major finding in our Systems Improvement Research studies and led us to target the following week for any feedback and analysis of data collected. And, over a period of time, we have found it very worthwhile to set up rotating teams of group members (usually three) to organize the data collection and analysis activity, with the total group participating under their direction. I hope these ideas have given you information you can use to make your group more effective, and that you have some fun carrying them out with your group.

---

[17]Ranking procedures and rank-order correlations are described in H. G. Dimock, *Simplified Guide to Program Evaluation*, pp. 53-58.

Interpersonal Skills Questionnaire

Hedley Dimock and Doug Scott

This questionnaire is to be used in describing a work colleague or associate. Circle the response which best describes how this person tends to behave.

	1 Rarely	2 Sometimes	3 Often	4 Most of the time	5 Almost always
1. This person is clear in describing his or her preferences and expectations for me and others.	1	2	3	4	5
2. This person is prepared to listen attentively to me when I am expressing my thoughts and feelings.	1	2	3	4	5
3. I can trust this person with my private ideas and opinions.	1	2	3	4	5
4. This person is sensitive and aware of how I am feeling in our mutual activities.	1	2	3	4	5
5. This person is open and flexible in implementing new ideas and proposals of others.	1	2	3	4	5
6. This person helps me feel included and supported in the group.	1	2	3	4	5
7. This person is open to receiving feedback on his or her behavior and its impact on me.	1	2	3	4	5
8. Personal concerns and problems of this person related to work are disclosed to me.	1	2	3	4	5
9. It is quite easy for me to have a talk with this person whenever I have the desire or need.	1	2	3	4	5

	1 Rarely	2 Sometimes	3 Often	4 Most of the time	5 Almost always
10. When I go to this person with a problem about my work, I know I'll get thoughtful criticism and constructive help.	1	2	3	4	5
11. This person's manner makes it easy for me to tell him or her when things aren't going as well as expected.	1	2	3	4	5
12. This person gives me commendation and recognition for a job well done.	1	2	3	4	5
13. This person is ready to confront me and others and deal with any possible conflicts.	1	2	3	4	5
14. When we are discussing group problems, this person asks for my ideas and opinions.	1	2	3	4	5

BIBLIOGRAPHY

Cronbach, Lee J. *Designing Evaluations of Educational and School Programs*, San Francisco: Jossey-Bass, 1982.

Cronbach, Lee J. *Essentials of Psychological Testing* (3rd edition), New York: Harper & Row, 1970.

Dimock, Hedley G. *A Simplified Guide to Program Evaluation*, Montreal: Centre for Human Relations and Community Studies, Concordia University, 1979.

Dimock, Hedley G. *The Dimock Leadership Inventory*, Sheridan Psychological Services, Box 6101, Orange, California 92667 (1970).

Gronlund, Norman E. *Measurement and Evaluation in Teaching* (3rd edition), New York: Macmillan, 1976.

Gronlund, Norman E. *Sociometry in the Classroom*, New York: Harper & Row, 1959.

Ligon, Ernest M. *Dimensions of Character*, New York: Macmillan, 1956.

Miles, Matthew B. *Qualitative Data Analysis*, Beverly Hills, CA: Sage, 1984.

Patton, Michael Quinn. *Qualitative Evaluation Methods*, Beverly Hills, CA: Sage, 1980.

Selltiz, Claire and others. *Research Methods in Social Relations* (5th edition), New York: Holt, Rinehart and Winston, 1984.

Smith, G. Milton. *A Simplified Guide to Statistics* (4th edition), New York: Holt, Rinehart and Winston, 1970.

Thorndike, Robert L. and Elizabeth Hagen. *Measurement and Evaluation in Psychology and Education* (4th edition), New York: John Wiley, 1977.

Part 4:
Planning Group
Development

Chapter 9

Planning Strong, Productive Groups

The full use of the concepts and understandings about developing healthy groups, and the skills of group observation and analysis that have been described, is dependent on a thoughtful planning process. This planning process is the key to actualizing all our knowledge and skill and helping groups become stronger and more effective. The six basic concepts of developing strong groups are the backbone of what we want to accomplish in our groups. The analysis of a group based on observations, peer nominations, and other data collection methods helps us understand its strengths and weaknesses. The planning process puts these together so we know what to do next with the group that is likely to be most helpful.

Developing Strong Groups

1. Recruit members who will be attracted to the group;

2. Set clear and attainable group goals;

3. Establish structures and rules to ensure that the goals will be accomplished;

4. Encourage teamwork and the sharing of leadership;

5. Demand that members invest significant time and energy in the group; and then

6. Make them aware of their personal contribution to the group's success.

Figure 20

Some or all of the six basic components in building strong, productive groups may happen naturally or on a chance, fortuitous basis. For example, recruiting members who will be attracted to the group may happen naturally if these people come and ask you to join the group. In reality this is unlikely to happen as studies (Zander, 1977) have suggested that in most groups 90

165

percent are asked to join. The role of the worker is to help the group improve its recruitment process through a systematic planning process. If the group is left to natural development processes it has no need for a professionally trained worker, as an administrative assistant or volunteer from the group could serve just as well. The professional worker helps the group use a planning process to relate their goals to action-taking based on extensive training in group theory and skills. Or, as I once heard an agency director tell her staff, "Anyone who hasn't got time for planning had better consider another career, as that person will not be working here very long."

Readers at this point likely are anxious to actualize their understanding of group growth and effectiveness and use a planning process to put their knowledge and skills to work for the good of the group. It is possible that their supervisor or colleagues may not share this orientation to planning. Planning may be resisted by suggesting "Let's keep it spontaneous and flexible," "We'll just play it by ear," or "Let's just go with the flow." These are usually strategies to maintain or increase control of the group and end up doing exactly what the person wanted to do in the first place. Spontaneous behavior ends up being more self-centered and controlling than reflective behavior, which is more likely to consider others. By avoiding planning, leaders do not have to present their preferred plans of action to the group and thus, they eliminate the possibility that others will modify or reject their plans. In other words, "going with the flow" is a strategy for keeping your ideas and plans hidden until the last minute when it is likely too late for others to interfere with what you want to do.

Planning helps us clarify our goals and intentions—what it is we want to do and why we want to do it. In this way planning helps to improve the choice of a particular action or behavior by stressing the possible choices and the likely impact of each alternative. A regular planning process also increases the likelihood that participants will be involved in making the plans and, therefore, the action or program will reflect their interests and preferences.

ASSUMPTIONS ABOUT REVITALIZING GROUPS

The planning process is considerably strengthened if it incorporates some basic assumptions about revitalizing groups. These assumptions are based on current social psychology understandings and have been fine-tuned in twelve years of Systems Improvement Research studies (Dimock, 1978, 1981).

Group Involvement in Planning

The more members are involved in setting goals for the group and planning for the revitalization of their group, the more likely it is to happen successfully and effectively. Participating in the data collection, decision-making, and implementation process changes group standards and creates self-induced motivational forces toward group goals. Planning for a group's development or revitalization requires the participation of members wherever it is feasible and practical. A key role of the group worker in guiding this planning process is to facilitate member involvement.

The Group, Not Individuals, Is the Focus for Improvements

The problems of a group are often associated with the individual members in the group. "If we only had a more effective chairperson, this group would really hum." "Why can't we get motivated members who would volunteer for some of the work that needs to be done?" But, changing the membership may not change the group. Consequently, the target for improvement should be the group's culture—its norms and standards. The theory supporting this assumption clarifies that individual behavior is closely related to the norms or standards of the group. Since the norms are the property of the group as a whole, they cannot easily be changed except by the group as a whole. This principle again emphasizes the need to involve the whole group in the planning process.

Reducing Blockages to Change

Group improvements are more easily accomplished by reducing the factors blocking them than by emphasizing the factors supporting them. In any group development plan there are always a number of reasons why it makes sense and should be implemented. But, there are often an equally large number of reasons why the proposed improvement may fail or bring harm to the group. Using this assumption suggests that the group consider and carefully analyze all the drawbacks to their revitalization plans, and try to overcome them, before implementing the plan.

Revitalization Spin-off

Implementing action plans for a group's improvement usually has an impact on areas related to the actual change. Each dimension of a group's life is interrelated to the other dimensions, and change in one area may produce repercussions in other areas that may require additional attention. Thus, a change in the attractiveness and successes of a group may increase its status so much that flocks of new people try to gain membership. This may pressure the group unduly to increase its size or split into two groups to accommodate the new members. Changes in group goals or programs may have repercussions on frequency of meetings, cost of operating the group, or physical space and resources needed. Paraphrasing Newton's third law of motion: "For every action in one part of a group, there may be an equal reaction in another part of the group." The guiding principle here is that the group development or revitalization planning process is a continuous one. If the planning concludes when one set of improvements have been made, the results will not be maximized and they will "wither on the vine."

Planning Group Improvements

1. Involve the group in the planning process.
2. Focus the planning on the group as a whole.
3. Work at reducing the blockages to improvements.
4. Make the planning a continuous process.

Figure 21

STRATEGIES FOR REVITALIZING GROUPS

During the planning process there are a number of strategies for revitalizing the group that are worth considering. They may be used singly or in combination and modified to suit the particular needs of the group.

1. *New experiences are provided.* These new experiences are expected to do a better job of meeting members' needs or of establishing procedures for improving group planning. New programs or activities may also be introduced which will increase cooperation, build trust and acceptance, or open up communication in the group. Field trips, visiting and observing

other similar groups, may provide these new experiences. They may also be built from resources within the group, demonstrations put on by the worker, or from outside resources (movies, handbooks, video presentations, or experts in the field).

2. *New information or values are presented.* These often take the format of a training program with lectures, audiovisual presentations, case studies, simulations, role plays, and demonstrations. Background reading and individual or group application projects may be used to round out this strategy. It is typical of experiences in school, leadership training programs, character education church programs, the scouts, and many informal adult education programs.

3. *Communication is improved by building a climate of trust and acceptance.* The group works at encouraging fuller participation and accepting or tolerating a wider variety of points of view. Trust is built as members experience their ideas receiving serious consideration. This increases their readiness to share their resources with the group and increases their commitment to group activities.

4. *Frustration energy from the group is refocused.* Negative energy emanating from unmet individual needs and the group's poor performance can be redirected into the planning for the group's improvement. Surfacing members' frustration and dissatisfaction with the present state of the group can be a powerful motivator to revitalization planning. Member dissatisfaction is most easily identified through group surveys and, as the results are shared with the group and members realize they are not alone in their dissatisfaction, common interests are identified. These common interests can be converted to new group goals which are likely to be enthusiastically pursued by members.

5. *The high-status or power members of the group can be used to give leadership to the revitalization planning.* Key members may be identified through peer ratings or sociograms and asked to lead task forces or chair special planning groups on revitalization planning. Key members may also be selected for advanced training outside the group (regional or national training events) and asked to help the group use the new skills and insights they learn.

6. *The relationship between the group and its environment may be changed.* Often, changing the physical location where the group meets, or the time of day, frequency of meetings, agency relationship, or interaction with other related groups supports or actualizes group revitalization plans.

7. *Insights into the group's development are explored.* Theories of group development which summarize the experiences of many other groups may

help a group put its own experiences into perspective. This strategy combines some kind of a group assessment or process analysis with current group development theory input to help the group compare its present state with other groups. The comparisons may help the group appreciate that its frustration with the worker or its planning procedures are a normal stage of development. More appropriate targets for group improvement may be identified as the group identifies the characteristic of a more advanced level of development.

PLANNING GROUP DEVELOPMENT

The systematic planning process for group development consists of the six phases listed below. As it is meant to be an ongoing process, replanning starts again as the results of the previous round of planning are assessed.

1. Collecting group information.
2. Clarifying and analyzing.
3. Identifying areas for participative action.
4. Action planning for group involvement and change.
5. Carrying out the plans.
6. Assessing the results and replanning.

Collecting Group Information

In order to assess the present position of the group and identify areas in which improvements would be helpful, a certain amount of information about the group is required. The major sources of information that have been described in previous sections include:

- *Group records* such as minutes of meetings, narrative descriptions, attendance records, and lists of previous programs.
- *Information and assessments based on direct observation* such as the Survey of Group Development, Roles of Group Members, interaction diagrams, and check sheets.
- *Group descriptions by members* such as peer descriptions and sociograms, social relations indexes, member roles, and post-meeting questionnaires or inventories.
- *Self-descriptions and reports* such as needs assessments and interest finders, information sheets, general questionnaires, and experience reports.

In planning for the collection of group information, some choices are usually made about the most important things to find out about, with areas of lesser interest being held over for possible use in a future planning round. For the priority areas selected, three sources for the information are identified to permit triangulation and offer some assurance that the information is confirmable. A useful test in determining which areas should be studied is to ask, "What would we be doing differently if we had that information?" How the information could be utilized, if at all, is the key question.

Clarifying and Analyzing

An effort is made in this step to summarize the information collected and list the major strengths and weaknesses of the group. The aim is to sort out the information to help the worker and members focus on the group's basic dynamics and come up with some hunches about the influence of these dynamics on the group. These hunches can then form a background for setting some targets for improvements or areas of participative action.

Identifying Areas for Participative Action

Two or three targets for change are needed to give focus to the group development or revitalization plan. Attempting to do several things at the same time tends to diffuse group energy and is more likely to be a weakness than a strength. Groups are strengthened by setting clear and attainable goals. These clear goals for improvement make the assessing results stage much easier. Targets such as "decreasing dependence on the worker" and "increasing the participation of low-status members" are more useful than wanting to "decrease flight behavior" or "increase the cohesion of the group." It may be helpful to make some goals very clear in measurable terms, such as "to recruit five new members" or "achieve an 85 percent attendance average during the next four meetings."

Action Planning for Group Involvement and Change

Following a clarification of the group's strengths and weaknesses and the identification of a couple of goals for improvement, the worker proceeds to involve the group in planning the next steps in action taking. The planning should consider the six components in developing strong groups (Figure 20) and the four principles for planning group improvements (Figure 21).

While it is important to have specific goals and objectives and a definite plan, these should not be set up in a way that limits flexibility, and some adaptations can be made as the group puts them into action. This flexibility can be encouraged by having "choice points" built into the plan which may lead to minor modifications.

Probably the most important role in action planning is to check for member commitment and enthusiasm in carrying out the proposed action plans. In the long run, member enthusiasm is more important than the quality or specificity of the plans. The major goal in revitalizing a group is to increase member attraction and enthusiasm for the group, and if the action plans leave the members uncertain, this goal is unlikely to be achieved.

If the actions are very involved, a tentative timetable or critical path plan for implementation will be beneficial. Resources outside the group that are required in the plan should be noted, their feasibility ascertained, and procedures set in motion to have them available at the called-for time.

Carrying Out the Plans

The implementation of the plans couples the involvement of the group in the implementation process with the achievement of the targeted goals. It can be difficult to keep a balance between these two forces. Sometimes, as the new ways of working get underway, the group's enthusiasm dwindles and it simply hopes that its objectives will be achieved. And, sometimes the group gets so caught up with its renewed involvement and enthusiasm that it wants to spend its time processing how it is working and neglects the goal it set out to accomplish. The worker may be needed to help the group maintain a healthy perspective and keep an appropriate balance of task and group forces at this critical time.

If the most important role of the team leader or group worker is to help the group set clear and attainable goals, then surely the second most important role is to make sure the goals are attained. The implementation of plans phase is a very busy period for the worker with continuous monitoring of implementation and helping the group get feedback on how things are going. Thus, if things are not going well, the group will be getting this feedback and will have ample opportunity to modify the plans before it is too late.

Our understanding of the revitalization and change process emphasizes that resistance to any new ways of working is often greatest just as the implementation gets underway and shows some signs of working well. Resistance is decreased if all members are continuously involved in the change process and there are frequent opportunities to discuss their problems and concerns.

Assessing Results and Replanning

While the focus of the assessment is on how well the action plans are working out, this is usually done in the context of a comprehensive review of the group's major dynamics. The most straightforward method is to collect again the kind of group information which was collected for the original planning. Then, the data from the survey of group development, roles of group members, sociograms, etc., can be compared and growth noted. The added advantage of the comprehensive survey is that changes in areas other than those planned for can be quickly picked up. These changes may be spin-offs from the planned change or regular development in the other areas.

Once it is felt that the plans have been implemented and that the new ways of working are firmly in place, it is time to use the feedback and evaluation information being collected to set some new targets for growth and improvement. These new targets may be second-priority items left over from the first round or they may be new targets more related to the spin-off (both strengths and weaknesses) of the changes occurring from the first round.

Integrating Planning into Normal Procedures

Like anything new, the planning procedures I have described tend to be stilted and artificial when first used by a group. They may tend to decrease the spontaneous, creative element of the group. This will pass as the procedures become a normal part of group life and the planning routine can become the group's first experiment with planned group development.

The planning for the group's development often takes a "problem" focus and this creates two difficulties. First, looking for problems may be inappropriate if the group is functioning smoothly and moving along well. The second difficulty is the feeling the group and the worker can have that if there are no "problems" then they don't need to continue with their planning—that their work on the group's development is done. Both of these are errors and it is better to keep the focus on "areas in which an improvement would increase group growth and member satisfaction."

PLANNING OUTLINE

I. Collecting Group Information

General information includes:

    1. Background information on the group.
    2. Background information on individual members.

3. A description of group activities.
4. How they planned and reacted to these activities.
5. How members functioned as a group.
6. Functions of individual members.
7. A view of the worker's roles and relationships in the group.

Data collection procedures:

1. Survey of group development.
2. Social relations scale, sociogram, or peer nominations.
3. Thumbnail sketches of members.
4. Observation reports (roles of group members, steps in problem solving, Group Observation Guide).
5. Interest finders.
6. Narrative records, anecdotal records.
7. Behavioral descriptions or behavior frequency check list.
8. Post-meeting reactions, member descriptions or evaluations of program.

II. Clarifying and Analyzing

1. What are the major strengths and weaknesses of the group?
2. What are the important factors affecting the group at this time?
3. How would you summarize the developmental phase of the group?
4. How do you analyze the factors holding the group back?

III. Identifying Areas for Participative Action

List the two or three major changes which would most likely revitalize the group and encourage its development (review Figure 20, Developing Strong Groups, and Survey of Group Development for ideas).

1. (Describe briefly and try to include some measurable objectives.)
2. (Describe briefly and try to include some measurable objectives.)
3. (Describe briefly and try to include some measurable objectives.)

Double check that these targets for change are both clearly stated goals and are attainable.

IV. Action Planning for Group Involvement and Change

In working out flexible plans to encourage growth in the target areas identified, the following guidelines are helpful:

1. Does the change focus on the group as a whole?
2. How can the group's acceptance and commitment for the change be gained?
3. What will be the form and extent of the group's involvement in making the change?
4. What are the factors supporting and resisting the change? (A force-field diagram might help here.) Can the plans reduce the forces against change? How will resistance to the change be handled?
5. What outside resources will be needed?
6. Can other areas that the change will affect be identified now?
7. What interventions will you make to facilitate and support the change?

V. Carrying Out the Plans

The carrying out of the plans may do one or several of the following:

1. Provide new experiences or training.
2. Provide new information.
3. Improve communication by building trust and acceptance.
4. Mobilize group energy into more effective patterns.
5. Alter the group's environment (physical, social, or organizational).
6. Redistribute power and leadership.

VI. Assessing Results and Replanning

This phase consists of repeating the information collection procedure from phase I and adding any that are related to the measurable objectives described in phase III. It is very important at this time to make sure that all the members have an opportunity to see this assessment feedback and, by reviewing the information and discussing it in the group, become very aware of their personal contribution to the group's success.

To the extent the targets for change were not fully accomplished, they may be reviewed as part of the group's analysis and setting of new targets for group improvement. It may be that the group will think it can still accomplish more in the originally identified areas and want to take a second crack at them. Or, it may feel its efforts have reached the point of diminishing results and decide to go to other areas. A measurable result of the full achievement of this phase is the group's acceptance of the planning process as a regular, routine activity of the group.

A CASE STUDY OF GROUP IMPROVEMENT

To get an idea of how some of this planning might go, let's take a fairly typical situation and work it through. The group we'll put together, based on the experiences of many groups, is a task force of eleven university students working on possibilities for student summer employment. They have a resource person from the university placement service and one from the dean of students' office. Both of the resource people worked with a similar group last year.

Collecting Group Information

The information on the group consisted of a survey of group development completed by the resource workers, the secretary's minutes of meetings, data from a brainstorming session on how the members thought they should do their jobs, and the academic records of the members. The minutes, including the meeting's attendance and a record of the group's election (chairperson and secretary), showed the friendship patterns within the group. Following four meetings (held twice a week), the resource people met with the chairperson and secretary to plan for the next few meetings of the group. They looked over the information they had and came up with the following analysis.

Clarifying and Analyzing

The five men and six women had all volunteered for the task force on summer employment and all but one had above average academic records. Most had experience in other student groups and all but three knew over half of the group previously. Attendance had been excellent except for one member who was on the basketball team and missed two meetings because of practices. Group morale was high and a strong cohesiveness was evident. The resource people were well accepted by the students.

On the less positive side the group members did not seem clear about their task and their specific responsibility for it. Along this line they tended to look to the resource people for direction saying, "What did the group do about this last year?" The secretary reported that he had a hard time getting things down as the discussion went in circles. The chairperson intervened frequently trying to get some clarity and agreement from the group about their goals. Three members were identified as playing non-functional roles but as these were of a joking around nature, some felt it helped to keep the meetings on a light note.

In summarizing these strengths and weaknesses, the members agreed that they had gotten off to a good start and were a pretty solid, cohesive group. But they felt that if they didn't increase their productivity and have something to show for their efforts, the group would start to sink.

Identifying Areas for Participative Action

1. *Set clear and measurable goals and objectives.* (As the goals were set, measurable objectives would be defined for each goal.)

2. *Improve problem-solving and decision-making procedures.* (Use observers to compare effectiveness using the Problem Solving Guide observation sheet.)

3. *Decrease dependence on the resource people.* (Monitor requests to resource people for help and the frequency of their giving direction to the group roles.)

Action Planning for Group Involvement and Change

The group set up task group A composed of the chairperson, secretary, and two advisors to work up a draft statement of goals and related measurable objectives, and to circulate the draft to all group members before the next meeting. Each member agreed to go over the goals, modify them or add new ones, and bring the results to the next meeting. At that meeting the modifications and changes would be discussed and the task force asked to rework their goals statement accordingly to incorporate the new ideas. At the following meeting the revised statement would be presented and checked for agreement with the group.

Plans for the second target for group improvement focused on a special half-day training session designed to improve skills and procedures in decision making. A colleague of the advisor from the dean of students' office, who had advanced training in improving group meetings, was recruited as a resource person to conduct the training session. This person was also asked to attend the session following the half-day training (when the group's goals would be decided on) to help the group use the skills and procedures learned in the training session. Two members volunteered to become task force B and work with the resource person in designing the training session and work as process observers during following meetings to ascertain how the learning was being applied.

Regarding the third target for group improvement (decreased dependence on the advisors), the group did not make any specific plans. It was felt that after the target had been discussed and agreed upon, then everyone was alerted to the concern. The advisors would try to reduce their direction giving and the members would try to increase taking responsibility themselves. The group also felt that as the group's goals became clearer and more specific and their procedures for working on them more effective (targets one and two), there would be less need to look to the advisors for direction.

Carrying Out the Plans

The overall strategy was to involve the members in the goal-setting activity and in the training session. The use of six people on the two task forces was expected to strengthen their sense of responsibility. Bringing in an outside resource person to help with the training session was hoped to lessen dependence on the two advisors. Training in new roles and skills would mobilize the group's energy into more effective procedures. And, the chairperson and secretary representing high-status members (as they were elected by the group) were used to legitimize and give support to the goal-setting activity. Adding the two advisors to task force A also used their status and influence to support and facilitate the goal-setting activity.

Assessing Results and Replanning

Assessment procedures were related to the measurable objectives for each of the three targets for improvement. Monitoring the results of the planning over the next six meetings showed a noteworthy revitalization of the group as the new goals fell into place and gave some clear direction to the group. And, the training in decision making led to much more productive meetings.

In the process it was found that the member who was on the basketball team made that group his priority and was asked to leave the group because of his absenteeism. The advisor from the university placement service also felt that as the group took over its own direction, there was little need for her and she resigned from the group.

New targets for group improvement were set around sharing more of the work load. Expectations for members' time and energy for implementing plans were increased and, while the chairperson continued to give general leadership to the group, the role of secretary was reassigned every four meetings.

Having a group process observer(s) was found to be very helpful and following the tenure of the task group B observers, two new observers were assigned for a period of four meetings. Continuous planning and feedback became a small but regular part of the group's activities.

Chapter 10

Group Development at Work

The extent to which a group is able to achieve its goals and enhance the satisfaction and personal growth of its members is greatly influenced by the way members are recruited or selected and the group is formed. The leadership style and model the worker presents to the group is also a major influence on its productivity and member morale. The way in which the group is formed—its size, composition, homogeneity, and compatibility—will greatly affect its cohesion and effectiveness. And, the status of the group—its attractiveness in the eyes of its participants—is also very important. The worker's behavior and way of working with the group, the amount of dependence developed, and the quality of the interpersonal relations established with members are more influential to the group's growth than any other intervention the worker is likely to make.

FORMING STRONG GROUPS

Recruit Members Who Will Be Attracted to the Group

People are looking to groups to meet many various needs, such as friendship, skill training, health, fun, help, status, and recognition. The more a group can meet a new member's needs, the more important and attractive the group will be and the stronger will be the membership of that person. If that member's needs change over a period of time and the group is seen as unable to meet them, leaving the group will be considered.

Forming a strong group depends on recruiting members who will be attracted to the group as it does a good job of meeting their needs. Upgrading a recruitment program depends on clearly outlining the needs the group can meet and then looking for the people who have those needs and interests, or, if potential members are readily available, then screening the applicants carefully to determine which ones are most likely to have important needs met by the group. Potential members, even young children, do a capable job of self-selection if they are given the information about what the group does, what it expects from members, and what members are likely to get out of the group experience. The selection process may also be improved by asking potential members what they hope to get out of the group and why that is important to them.

Many agencies feel they have very little say about who joins their programs and these recruitment ideas may not seem relevant. Continuing to develop the rationale may show what can be done once they are members to maximize the potential attraction of the group. The idea is the same; the more the members think the group could meet important needs for them, the more they will see the group as attractive and worthy of their time and energy. This might be done by conducting a needs and interests survey of members and then showing how group activities will meet these needs. Some redesign of program or usual ways of working may enable the group to meet more of the identified needs. Anything that can be done to increase the importance of the needs the group can fill will also be helpful. Emphasizing the many applications of a particular skill or the values of new friendships are examples. A group can also heighten its appeal to members by providing direct feedback to members on how well it is doing in meeting their needs. This suggests some kind of a regular review of members' objectives and what the group is providing. Some groups do this by having members put their own "Give" and "Gets" list on newsprint, hang it on the wall, and then review it in the group. This could be adapted to a "Wants" and "Gets" list. Members who find large discrepancies between what they want and what they get are likely to be unhappy and reduce group strength and effectiveness. They should be encouraged, and perhaps helped, to move on to other activities or groups.

Some rules of thumb in forming groups include the following:

1. *Friendship choices.* "Birds of a feather flock together," and the more we can get a flock into a group, the stronger the group will be. In the old days, Y's, Boys Clubs, and neighborhood houses recruited groups of friends from school or the same street and formed them into a group. Like intact neighborhood gangs, they had tremendous group strength. Companies in Japan recruit friends from the same school and put them to work in the same departments. The results are excellent, and when supported by a variety of other measures we'll discuss later, result in groups of lifelong company employees. Studies consistently show that members participate in a group much more, and likely have more personal satisfaction, when it is composed

of friends. Even in situations where people know each other very little, such as campers at the first day of camp or participants attending a workshop, groups composed of individual choices do better than those formed by random assignment.

2. *Similarity.* Continuing the theme of "birds of a feather flock together," similarity among members is an obvious consideration in forming groups. However, the important kind of similarity is in goals, aspirations, attitudes, and beliefs. Age, grade, or intelligence similarity have little relation to group cohesion. Why then, you ask, are so many groups formed on the basis of age, grade, or intelligence? This practice is a holdover from the days when those factors were thought to be important and they are continued chiefly because they are easy and convenient for workers to use. For example, the practice of separating grade school youth into groups based on their ability is still used although research has shown it is counterproductive, yet it appears to many educators an easier way to handle differences and work on material of common interest. Camps typically establish groups on the basis of age, and recreation programs have beginner, intermediate, and advanced levels.

Another misunderstanding of the value of similarity is to group people according to illness, presenting problem, physical ability, geographical area, work background, and other artificial categories. The real issues should be common goals and attitudes. But, most people have accepted or even built up expectations to be in special groups and, as they are very convenient, most human service organizations form many of their groups along these lines. This may give a social agency a group of teenage mothers and another group of single parents. It is unlikely they will have any contact with each other although the teens could learn a great deal from the older, experienced parents, and the older parents might really "get their act together" when they were trying to help the teen group. Composing groups based on these kinds of similarities may help in recruiting and initially attracting group members, but may reduce learning and personal growth.

3. *Ability and skill.* Participants are most attracted to groups where the skill and ability of the other members is seen as equal to or greater than their own. There is a special attraction to a group of winners or champions—a group thought to be the best of its kind. Interests and skills may also be related to common goals and, therefore, a powerful contributor to attraction and cohesion. Athletic teams, technical skill training groups, and special interest recreation groups, such as classes in ceramics or skiing, are most attractive when composed of people with similar aspirations.

4. *Gender and race.* The concept that similarities attract applies to gender and race. At least initially, homogeneity of gender or race seems to

be an attraction to a group. But, once the group is underway, the similarity of aspirations and the mixture of diverse yet relevant activities (Thelen's concept of least group size) takes over as more important. It is clear that men and women behave differently in mixed groups than in single-sex groups and research interest in these differences has increased rapidly in the last few years. However, mixed groups have generally been found to be more effective than single-sex groups.

Racial groups prefer to interact with their own race, and even in racially integrated situations, such as schools, neighborhoods, and the armed forces, this preference prevails. Mixed racial groups tend to create interpersonal tension and members behave differently. However, after that initial phase it appears to me that the book is open and my hunch is that we'll find friendships, similar attitudes, and aspirations to be the more relevant factors.

Mixed groups are quite natural for youth of all ages as witnessed by their spontaneous formation on the streets and in the playgrounds. At different stages of development, boys and girls prefer to be in groups of their own sex. Human service organizations can provide for these changing interests and needs by leaving the gender question open by allowing single-sex, mixed, and brother or sister groups (single-sex groups with a lot of combined programs) to form. The needs or preferences of the workers are also important, and in many organizations and especially institutions, single-sex groups are formed to meet their needs, expectations, and biases. Single-sex groups are often believed to be less dynamic, more submissive, easier to manage, and perhaps more moral; staff members decide for the participants along these lines.

Other Considerations in Group Formation

Problem members or those who appear to have different behavioral patterns from other members are a great concern to workers forming new groups. These members may share the same aspirations as others but may be more self-centered, disturbed, or aggressive than others. There is often a concern, especially with youth groups, that a "rotten apple will spoil the barrel." Normally healthy children and adults are quite safe, as they are secure in their own behavior and have no attraction for the different or antisocial behavior presented by the problem member. On the contrary, a normal group is likely to be a strong, positive influence on a problem member if that person has a reasonably strong attraction to the group. People may be superficially categorized as misfits and put together in the same group assuming they have a similarity. This is not likely to work out unless the group finds common goals or aspirations around which it can build.[18]

Recruitment Strategies

Recruiting new members and removing old ones are the two most critical processes in maintaining the very existence of the group. Poorly formed groups can easily become weak, apathetic groups that require a great deal of staff time to keep going. Attention to recruiting and selecting members deserves considerable time and attention. Some strategies for improving recruitment include the following suggestions:

- Identify as a target population those people likely to have attitudes, values, and aspirations similar to present group members.
- Have friends approach the potential recruits or recruit friends in two's or three's.
- Use pairs of members to visit potential recruits. (They can support each other and reflect different aspects of the group.)
- Talk to the recruits about the benefits they will receive from joining (new skills; opportunity to use old skills, make new friends, accomplish personal goals, contribute to others, earn money or recognition, have fun, be important or a leader; personal development).
- Clarify and stress areas of common attitudes, values, and aspirations (to show that the recruits will be compatible and accepted by the group, and that others will value their input).
- To increase the perceived status and prestige of the group, talk about its recent successes, and describe the position and status of the present members. Stress the high level of skills they have.

---

[18]During my camp days, there were several boys who were seen as misfits, and the director was reluctant to place them in regular cabin groups. A careful look at these boys, who had an age range of several years, revealed that they were all very interested in dramatics. A new cabin was built next to the camp theater and a very cohesive and successful group was built around the common goal of putting on camp plays.

- Involve the recruits slowly by asking them to do a small job for the group, such as referee a game, help out with an art auction, or make a short presentation to the group. (Assume that minor involvement will demonstrate the appealing qualities of the group.)
- Have the recruits sit in on a group session. (Seeing the other members increases the possibilities for attraction based on physical attractiveness, attitude similarity, and common goals or needs compatibility.)

Optimal Group Size

Maintaining an optimal size for the group based on sound recruitment of new members who have the talents for the work to be done, and dropping old members who are no longer contributing to the group, rounds out the powerful impact on a group of the recruitment process. Attitude similarity was a notable criteria for forming a strong group, as interactions are more likely to be satisfying when they support one's beliefs and opinions. In groups where people can interact frequently, there is likely to be more attraction to the group if there is this similarity.

The size of the group needs to be related to the goals, aspirations, and interaction requirements of the members. Natural groups do a good job of determining their own best size, for if they get too large, subgroups will form to participate in the activity. Most groups in human services have their size at least roughly determined by the staff, depending somewhat on the numbers seeking membership. The amount of "air time" for each member in a meeting, and the possibilities of interacting with all the other members should be worked out in establishing a size that will strengthen rather than weaken the group.

Group sizes of ten to twenty members provide reasonable interaction possibilities if the group meets for two hours at a time. Large groups would need to subdivide to provide the same interaction time and then it would not be with the total group. Yet, our experiences are filled with larger groups that year after year attract membership. And, certainly, it is an exciting experience to be in a parade of thousands, sing in a hundred-voice choir, or be present at a Billy Graham crusade with a quarter of a million people. While these groups are attractive, they are not as likely to be strong and cohesive.

It has been my experience that most groups in human service organizations are larger than the optimal size, as workers and members may feel that larger numbers make for more important groups. And, in recent times of a lean economy, more people per group appear to make it more cost-effective. Thus, there may be increased pressure to increase group size irrespective of the handicap this places on the strength and usefulness of the group. Probably the best "rule of thumb" on group size was proposed by Thelen[19] in his principle of *least group size*. This rule said that a group should be limited to the smallest number of people who could provide all the task and group-building resources needed to accomplish the group's goals. This is an optimal resource theory which suggests that groups assess what skills are needed for the particular activity or task of the group and then recruit members accordingly. The size of the group will be limited to the smallest number of people needed to provide these resources.

Suggested guidelines using these principles are:

- Cabin groups at camp—five to eight members.
- Therapy or personal growth groups—five to ten members.
- Club groups of youth—six to fifteen members.
- Boards of directors—eight to sixteen (maximum twenty) members.
- Human relations training or T-groups—ten to fifteen members.
- Experiential training groups—twelve to twenty (not more than 24) members.
- Classroom groups meeting for more than fifty hours at least twice a week—up to 30-35 members.
- Classroom groups of over 35 members should be broken down into work units of five to eight students.
- Teams and committees—smallest number needed for the activity or task of the group.

MAINTAINING STRONG GROUPS

Part 1 described a number of elements contributing to strong groups. These and other related factors are reviewed with several action implications proposed. The goal is to develop and maintain a strong group by making and keeping it attractive to the members. The key contributors to group attraction are personal need satisfaction and success in task accomplishment.

---

[19]Herbert A. Thelen, *Dynamics of Groups at Work*. Chicago: University of Chicago Press, 1954.

Getting Started

Physical and psychological proximity are important in helping a group build strength. Attention should be given to setting up the group's physical arrangements so that members will be close to one another. For example, desks in an office, lockers in a locker room, chairs in a meeting room, offices in an agency, or rooms in a dormitory should be arranged to encourage maximum interaction. Consideration should be given to having the group share the same large office rather than having small, separate offices. Residential training facilities use this concept in designing living quarters that are exceedingly small and shared by two people. The expectation is that trainees will spend little time separated in their rooms and will join others in a comfortable common room where group building can take place.

If it is not possible for the group members to share a physical proximity often (boards of directors, regional associations), then anything that gives a sense of closeness is helpful. Applications of this concept could include phone calls, memos, newsletters, and sharing ideas through questionnaires or position papers on relevant topics. Or, if the members are geographically separated, it may be possible to have them pair up or subgroup for certain tasks. A large electronics firm with whom I consulted had regional offices in four cities across the country. During one of our team-building activities, we had conference call meetings (everyone on the phone at the same time) every Monday morning. During the week the subgroups would meet again to plan for the next conference call. Telex memos and shared responses to forthcoming activities also contributed to the psychological proximity that helps to develop a stronger, more effective group.

The concept of optimal interaction states that the more members interact, the more likely they are to be attracted to one another. In applying this concept, groups will carefully consider the frequency and length of their meetings or joint activities as well as facilitating physical proximity. For example, regional meetings of the type used with the electronics firm were twice a year but needed to be two days in length to increase the strength of the group. Comparable minimums are a half- day (3½ hours) for once-a-month meetings, two hours for once-a-week meetings, and an hour for meetings or activities held three times a week. My preference is for a half-day a week or two hours two or three times a week.

The concept of group distinction ascertains that members of a group will feel more cohesion if they see their group as separate and distinct from other groups. The first possibility of applying this concept is to provide the group with their own separate space—meeting room, play area, floor in a dormitory or housing unit, or workshop—and then putting their name on it to highlight its separateness.

Other ways to establish a group's distinction are to give it a special name; group hats, sweaters, insignia pins, crests, badges, or uniforms (jackets, scarves, arm bands); unique stationery; a pennant or flag; or specially marked parking spaces, eating tables, tools, cars, and equipment. It amazes me to see how long people will carry a notebook or folder with a group's insignia or special meeting noted on it. Obviously, these are much more important status and identity givers than some of us realize.

In getting started or in admitting new members a group will enhance its attractiveness if it appears that the group is selective in choosing members—that only special people belong. Establishing some kind of initiation or investiture ceremony is one way of doing this. A group also does well to have some sort of an orientation experience or pre-induction training program to extend this perception that membership in the group is special. The induction ceremony may then be as simple as presenting the new members to the group with perhaps a short biographical sketch and then giving them some sort of special welcome as full-fledged members. The group's unique pin, crest, hat, or jacket would be presented, and if there is a group song, motto, creed, or handshake, it would be used at this time.

Setting Clear and Attainable Goals

A group is strengthened to the extent that it has clear goals and every member knows what his or her role is in helping to achieve them. Most individuals and groups, if left to themselves, set goals that are either too high, or they underestimate the time it will take to accomplish them. Failure to achieve goals leads to frustration, disappointment, and a disenchantment with the group. Nobody likes to be a loser or associate with losing teams or groups. For groups to develop and maintain strength, they must experience reasonable success in accomplishing their goals.

High goals are usually seen by members as providing more pride and satisfaction than low goals. And, if a group does not achieve its goal, it usually leaves it the same rather than lowering it. Thus, goals continue to escalate or stay the same and groups fail to reach these goals more often than they succeed. The following procedures help groups to set clear and attainable goals.

1. Once the group goal has been clearly defined, ask one of the least involved members to summarize it. If it is now well described, ask others for their understanding. (Sounds simple, but wait until you try it.)

2. Ask the group to review their previous experiences and establish their "track record" on the goal they are setting. (Accurate measures of the group's performance in the past should be the basis for setting new goals.)

3. Once the group has set its goal and the time line for accomplishing it, propose periodic, formal check-in points to assess progress toward the goal and revise it if indicated. (This is the concept of continuous, immediate feedback to reassess goals and performance. In my consultations I build "change of scope" reports on a periodic basis with a minimum of one halfway through, to assess accomplishments and consider revising goals and timetable.)

4. If these periodic check-in points are accepted by the group, suggest a downward revision of the goal until the first review, indicating that if high success has been obtained, the goal can easily be revised upward.

5. If the group has set high and apparently unrealistic goals, ask that their goals be compared to the performance of other groups.

6. To the extent high and unrealistic goals may be related to external pressures, make sure the group devises a strategy for running interference on these pressures. For example, parents often pressure for unrealistic achievements in their youths' academic work or their athletic endeavors. Measures should be taken to cushion these pressures before they reach the group and distort goal setting.

Establishing Structures and Rules to Ensure the Goals Will Be Accomplished

Once the group has established realistic goals and they are clearly understood by all group members, it is time to shift attention to developing standards and procedures to make sure the goals are achieved. *Nothing succeeds like success.* All members need to know the part they play as individuals in helping the group accomplish its goals. The group has established a number of informal rules which help the members work together in accomplishing its tasks. When these rules or norms are well known, members know what is expected of them and the other members, which behaviors will merit rewards and which will be punished.

Some basic rules or norms are around attendance, hours of work or practice, and who gets to decide what for whom. Groups may set up formal structures for these expectations but they do not have as much relevance as what the group informally enforces. For example, a group may be scheduled to meet once a week for three hours. The informal norms that are important are: How many meetings is a member allowed to miss before the group puts on pressure to be there? What time will the meeting really start and finish? Team practices may see everyone working out before the formal starting time, and board members may continue for an hour or two after the stated closing time. Members need to know how decisions are going to be made and the usual practices or procedures for operating the group.

The group norm about absences is particularly influential on group strength, for if members aren't there, they can't interact with others and increase their interaction with the group. The members present must pick up the slack created by absentees and probably spend additional time bringing them up to date when they return. Consistent absenteeism also gives the impression that the group is not particularly important to its members and morale declines. Groups can prevent this from happening by establishing clear rules to which there is a high commitment to enforcing informally and making sure that everyone is clear about what will happen if they don't conform. Rotary Clubs insist that members attend every meeting or make them up at other clubs. And, some boards of directors require attendance at three out of four meetings.

Many important rules are developed very inconspicuously as the group gets started but after a few months become firmly entrenched as the usual ways of doing things. These may include a dress code, special privileges allowed, productivity expectations (goals scored by the team or length of agenda accomplished in student council meetings), what gets talked about in the group and what privately, how conflicts are handled, and the basis of group decisions (such as majority rule). Thus, it is critical to monitor the formulation of these standards during the early life of the group, and if they seem to be heading in an unproductive direction, verbally raise the rule in question so members can make it on a thought-out, logical basis. Otherwise, the accumulated practices will become "the way we have always dealt with that problem."

The actual structures and procedures that will contribute to the group achieving its goals depends very much on what these goals are. Teaching methods are important to classroom or training groups, decision-making procedures to boards of directors, skill-training practice to athletic teams, and program planning to friendship and activity groups.

Encouraging Teamwork and the Sharing of Leadership

Directive and coaching styles of leadership are most useful in the early life of the group as members are learning their roles and the skills related to goal achievement. As the group starts demonstrating its competence in using these skills, a more participative style which encourages the sharing of leadership is indicated. The development of a group and the maintenance of its strength is aborted if the leader or worker is not able to share control with the group.

Most human service workers have quite an investment in their technical skills and their self-esteem is built on their helping others learn these skills. They often feel they are not doing their job if they are not directly leading or coaching the group. Moving through the usual developmental phases of dependence, counterdependence, and interdependence with a group puts quite a strain on a leader. Yet, the worker who is successful in teaching the members the skills they need to run the group, and then allows them to take over the group and use them, appears to have worked himself or herself out of a job. A functional indicator that members are no longer dependent on their leader is when the leader misses a meeting and the meeting goes on the same as usual.

The ancient Chinese philosopher Lao-Tse said of a good leader that when his task is finished, his goal achieved, the people will say, "We did this ourselves." While this philosophy promotes group development to full maturity, it clearly reduces the importance of the worker's role in the group. Giving up the satisfaction of teaching and coaching a group is difficult, yet as workers develop more skills in delegating and listening, they may find a new source of satisfaction in watching the members use the skills they have learned to run the group themselves.

Clear group goals that are shared by the members are essential to building teamwork. The best way to facilitate the sense of shared goals is to have all the members participate in establishing them. Participation in goal setting also increases the probability that members will be clear about the goals and understand them fully.

Group goals are also more likely to encourage teamwork if all members are aware of what their part is in accomplishing them. There need to be clear and specific expectations for each member and the accountability that goes along with each member's role. Superordinate goals—those that can only be accomplished through contributions from all members—are most likely to enhance teamwork and the group's success.

Group goals or procedures that encourage competition among members are the most common blocks to teamwork. For example, the procedure of using a majority vote as the basis for decision making encourages competition (over half wins, the others lose) and works against teamwork. In Japanese quality circles, by contrast, all members participate in setting unit goals and no decisions are made until everyone agrees. Making decisions takes an unbelievable amount of time but the teamwork that results from the shared goals is also unbelievably effective.

Other activities that discriminate among the contributions of individual members decrease teamwork. Typical examples are school grades based on individual performance, volunteer-of-the-year awards, emphasizing the scoring of individuals rather than the team as a whole, and other forms of recognition that encourage members' competing with one another. While there may be considerable energy mobilized by these activities, and the performance of some members increased, the trade-off is in group cohesion and teamwork. The Japanese resolve this concern by relating salary only to seniority rather than productivity or performance. This is similar to a teacher's salary in North America being chiefly determined by years of experience.

Members need to know what the goals of the group are, exactly what they can do to contribute to these goals, how to do their particular contribution, and what the rewards or punishments will be related to their success. And, the more they feel that the goals can only be attained through the utilization of all the group's member resources, the higher will be their motivation to collaborate with others in achieving these goals.

Demanding Members Invest
Significant Time and Energy in the Group

The concept of least group size says a group should contain the smallest number of members needed to provide the skills and resources required for the group's activity. In practice, additional members are added to "share the load" and reduce the demands on any one member. This is especially the case in working with volunteers where the feeling is "if we ask too much of our volunteers, they will leave us." More likely the opposite is true, for members who have made a significant contribution of time and energy are much more likely to value the group and be attracted to it.

Zander (1982) goes beyond the "significant contribution" concept and says that major sacrifices made by members increase their attraction to the group. These sacrifices may be giving up a vacation, working overtime, foregoing a pay increase, or working on a weekend or holiday. Some fund-raising consultants appear to apply this concept when they ask all fund raisers to make their own contribution before they start campaigning, and suggest that prospects not be asked to give more than fund raisers. Asking members to make sacrifices for the group works best with those members already attracted to the group. This concept also fits in with our understanding of the initiation requirements of many groups where prospective members are required to make some sacrifice to gain admission. Officer candidates in the armed forces have to pass basic training, college fraternity pledges are expected to undergo physical and psychological torments, and country club applicants must pay a large initiation fee.

Participants in group activities, whether they are paying to belong to the group, are an unpaid volunteer, or a paid worker, all want to be known and recognized as members who have made important contributions to the group's success. Successful groups make sure they provide these opportunities for members to make meaningful contributions. If members are not used, they may feel they are not needed and their attraction to the group will decrease.

This "requiring an investment" is an important concept and, as it took me so long to learn it, I want to stress it. As director of group guidance at the Montreal Children's Hospital, I was responsible for volunteers. During my first year, I continued the practice of not asking too much from volunteers. Then, I started a three-week training program to qualify as a volunteer and established higher expectations for participation in hospital activities. The number of volunteers increased rapidly and their work hours and length of service did, too. Later, as a beginning consultant, I contributed my services to run training programs for financially pressed agencies, but few people would come to these free programs. Then, I started asking the agency to charge an admission fee for the programs and interest in them picked up dramatically. It appears that if nothing is asked of you, you give nothing—not even your attendance at a free program. But, even if some small sacrifice is required, you value that activity or program.

Making Members Aware of Their Personal Contribution to the Group's Success

People join groups in order to meet their needs, and the more they feel they are meeting these needs, the more important the group is to them. It is not sufficient just to meet needs; the members have to see or feel that the needs are met. And, an important need for most people is to feel that they are important to the group, that they regularly contribute to the group's success.

Regular reviews of group achievement or some kind of periodic feedback on progress toward goals is helpful. The feedback is most useful if it shows how each person contributed to the success of the group in fulfilling the goal. Members should be left with the feeling that their contribution was essential to the group achieving the goal rather than a competitive comparison that shows how much of the goal they personally achieved. Hopefully, members will find increased satisfaction from these successes of the group as a whole.

The move from an individual needs motivation to a group-oriented motivation is enhanced by high visibility of the group's success. The more widely a group's accomplishments are known, the more members can bask in its reflected glory. Raising the status and popularity of a group in the community is a sure way, too, of increasing its attractiveness to members. Members will then be more likely to work for the good of the group, as just belonging to such a special group brings considerable satisfaction. The more members are interested in their group's product, the more likely they are to begin assessing how well their group is performing as a whole.

Group goal setting and feedback on accomplishment is a joint, continuous process. Field studies have shown that members' desire for group success strengthens when they receive regular reports on how well the group did on a specific task. If the members attain the goal, they will derive satisfaction which stimulates interest in further successes. Over a period of time, a series of successes will generate a strong sense of pride in the group. This again emphasizes how important it is to set clear and attainable goals and then make sure the group achieves them. Proclaiming these successes and giving them wide visibility in the community makes everyone aware of them. Indicating to members how their personal contribution was vital to the group's success completes this group-building process. The group's success must be seen as dependent on the contribution of all its members.

Achievement proclamations and group recognition can take many forms. Their goal is to specify what the group accomplished, develop a sense of pride in the group by recognizing these accomplishments, and increase the group's status by letting others in the community know. Some usual methods are having a recognition banquet; publishing a special newsletter; celebrating with a picnic, wine and cheese party, or barbecue; giving recognition awards to all members, such as a certificate, pin, badge, hat, or other memento of the achievement; specific coverage and stories in the newspapers, radio, and TV; and a special meeting with a high-status dignitary (agency director, mayor, or outstanding person in the related field) who proclaims the achievements and gives them high visibility and status. Note that these activities are not in the style of an awards celebration where three or four high-achieving members are selected for special recognition of their personal accomplishments or contributions. Rather, the focus is on pride in the accomplishments of the group as a whole.

IMPROVING GROUP MEETINGS

Everyone has attended many useless, boring, if not frustrating meetings. There are so many ineffective meetings taking place that most people have come to expect very little from a planning or decision-making meeting. It is hard to believe that meeting chairpersons will spend fifteen minutes just before a meeting to sketch out a hasty agenda even though the meeting involves fifteen or more people and will last two or three hours. The same people will cheerfully spend hours preparing a short speech, days preparing an article for the agency newsletter, and weeks designing a training program for the same fifteen people.

But even for new staff who are enthusiastic about using participative leadership procedures where program participants will plan their own programs, the group decision-making process does not come easy. Planning a good meeting is like designing an exciting and educational training program—it takes a lot of time and know-how to do it well. Yet, few meeting planners have ever had any preparation or training for running an effective meeting.

Many years ago, when I was a consultant to the Montreal Y camp, I encountered a staff group who was anxious to have a participative camp and let the campers plan their own programs. I worked with the staff during their precamp training and then returned about two weeks after camp had started. The staff was frustrated and dismayed to find that decision making with youngsters was very difficult and they had few skills that were helpful. The next several sessions of our incamp staff training were devoted to decision-making skills and we all learned a great deal. My consulting work since then has reinforced this learning experience, that wanting to involve people in making the decisions which affect them has little value unless planners have the skills to facilitate the decision-making process.

Group planning sessions are the place to start "establishing structure and rules to ensure the goals will be accomplished." The critical role of group planning and the decision-making procedures that support it becomes the paramount focus of planners. A concept that has blocked appropriate planning suggests that the role of the chairperson in a democratic or participative group is to get the group together, throw them the ball, and let them work it out. Let's review our understanding of leadership in the context of group decision making.

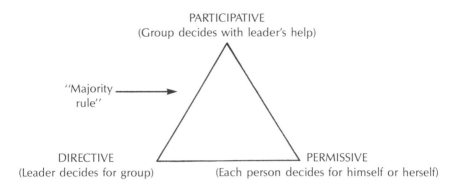

PARTICIPATIVE
(Group decides with leader's help)

"Majority ———————▶
rule"

DIRECTIVE
(Leader decides for group)

PERMISSIVE
(Each person decides for himself or herself)

In the participatory mode, the group decides with the leader or chairperson's help. In the permissive mode the leader withdraws or abdicates, modeling an "all members do their own thing" standard. Majority rule allows anything over half of the group to make a decision that is binding on everyone. Our diagram shows it just over halfway between one person deciding and the whole group deciding. This clarifies that it is about halfway between a directive or autocratic mode and a participative mode where the group works toward general agreement. This general agreement is not meant to be consensus where everyone has to agree or the decision won't be made. That would mean one person, by withholding a vote, could decide what the group won't do, which would be the same as the directive/autocratic mode where one person decides what the group will do.

The concept of throwing out a few decisions for a group to make and then taking a quick vote to decide them has little in common with participatory decision making. A majority decision tends to divide the group into winners and losers. It divides interests and loyalties in the group and encourages competition by having winners and losers. A group that works more in total agreement makes each member important by working toward full agreement for a group decision. Minority opinions are given more attention and this often raises the quality of decisions, as minorities may be creative group members. Working toward full agreement by encouraging consideration of everyone's ideas produces a secure and permissive climate, and exemplifies the teamwork needed to build a strong group.

Common Problems of Decision-Making Meetings

The most difficult problem planners have in getting ready for a meeting where important decisions will be made is to decide how much control to give the group in making the decision. They may have a favored decision which they really want to see happen. Or, they may fear the group may not make a very good decision and that it could take a long time to work it out. There may be concern that giving up control will make them appear weak and less competent as leaders. This can be an overwhelming concern for newly selected planners who feel unsure about their status and their ability to do the job. In groups where I am the responsible person, I am often concerned with how much control I am prepared to give the group, and if I let them decide this time, will it set an unworkable precedent for next time? The best way I have found to test my readiness to encourage a group to make a particular decision is to ask myself, "What is the worst possible decision the group could make?" If I feel I could accept that decision, if worst came to worst, then I can encourage the group to go ahead with its own decisions. If I think I could not accept it, then instead of pretending I am open and flexible, I express my concern or reservation to the group. There are often limits within which decisions can be made and it is important to describe them before starting rather than waiting until the group has made an unacceptable decision and then trying to veto it.

High-control decisions take less time, are deemed better by planners though they eliminate creative contributions by the group, but are not as likely to be implemented by the group. Clearly, there is a trade-off between having to go through a time-consuming and difficult group decision-making process and getting the commitment from members needed to ensure proper implementation of the decision.

Additional common problems include:

GROUP DECISION STYLES

	Strengths	Weaknesses
Planners Decide	High-quality decisions Clear focus and direction Minimum time expended	Creative contributions are eliminated No commitment to decision (implementation may be avoided)
Group Decides	Groups may be more creative High satisfaction with results Implementation assured	May take considerable time Decision may be inappropriate (at least to planners)

1. The chairperson plays an inadequate managing role.
2. The group does not use any systematic procedures, such as Logical Steps in Problem Solving.
3. The subject under discussion is outside the interests, ability, or area of control of the group.
4. Off-topic discussions arise and cloud the real concerns of the group.
5. After decisions are made, implementation plans are left up in the air.

Getting Ready for the Meeting

A problem-solving or decision-making session will be significantly improved if there is a chairperson or recognized discussion leader. Often, a moderately sophisticated group (especially my university students) makes a point of not having a chairperson—"we don't need one." This is an error, for research has demonstrated that problem-solving groups function more effectively with a chairperson. One study showed that groups where the chairperson had been selected on a random basis were more successful in solving problems than groups without a chairperson. Thus, a chairperson, even though his skills are no greater than those of other members, is better than no chairperson at all. The practice of rotating the chairperson among group members is well supported by this point of view.

Time is a typical problem in most group situations, as participative decision making takes a great deal of time. As it is frustrating to frequently run out of time while working on a decision, I suggest two approaches. First, save the group's planning time for only important decisions. Usually, the group can set priorities about what it wants to work on and how much time it is prepared to devote to that work. Secondly, allow more time for an agenda than it would appear to take. While "work may fill the time available for its completion," it is very satisfying to end a decision-making session ahead of time. Above all, organizational schedules that lock groups into a maximum of twenty to thirty minutes to plan a series of activities should be carefully avoided. Remember that our second principle of maintaining strong groups is to establish the structures and rules to ensure that the goals will be accomplished.

Everyone at the meeting needs to know what the goals for the meeting are, and the best way to do this is through a prepared meeting agenda. It is helpful if participants have had an opportunity for input into the preparation of the agenda and vital that they have it before the meeting. For best results, members should have at least the tentative agenda in their hands two days before the meeting. This enables them to look over any accompanying documents (record of the last meeting, position papers, financial report) and collect information they want to present regarding the topics listed on the agenda. In some organizations people will not attend a meeting if they don't have the agenda in advance, as they feel that without it, the meeting will be a waste of time.

Assuming the meeting will have a chairperson, the other half of the leadership team is a recorder. I use the term recorder rather than secretary to indicate a difference in focus. Secretaries are usually expected to keep minutes of the meeting, noting who said what on different topics and recording notes on decisions. The group recorder, in contrast, takes an active role in the meeting, helping the group keep its discussion on track and pointing out where it is in its sequence of problem-solving steps. The recorder notes the decision reached for each agenda item, the action required, who is responsible for implementation, and the date or time line for completion. The recorder keeps this information up to date and helps to prepare each meeting's agenda by preparing "reports of action required" for items from previous meetings. Thus, items discussed do not get lost in the shuffle or come up six months later to be discussed all over again. And, those people taking on implementation responsibilities know that a report from them will be expected on the date agreed on.

A group may call on the recorder to restate the development of the discussion to that time or to summarize the areas of agreement and disagreement. As part of the leadership team, the recorder as well as the chairperson may intervene to facilitate group procedures. If a member moves too quickly to start evaluating the proposed solutions to an issue, the recorder may ask if there are any more proposals before the group starts evaluation. The recorder shares the leadership load and may be quite active during meetings—in many ways a co-leader.

In making physical arrangements for the meeting, the planner will want to choose surroundings that fit the type of meeting and are appropriate both physically and psychologically. University students may feel very excited about meeting in the faculty club, but be unable to get down to business. A room that is conducive to work is evenly heated and well ventilated, with furniture placed so that everyone can see and hear what is taking place. A chalkboard or newsprint for visual presentations is a useful addition. A round table is most suitable for group discussions, but octagonal or triangular configurations are close seconds. In any case, all participants should be able to see each other. Groups meeting where there are frequent distractions are often unable to keep the attention of the members. This is a major drawback to meeting outdoors or near a place where other activity is in progress.

Using Logical Steps in Problem Solving

The use of logical steps in problem solving quickly improves the quality and efficiency of any group discussion. While the actual steps may vary, they are founded on a traditional, scientific method which suggests that you define a problem, collect data about the problem, make a hypothesis about the origin of the problem or how the problem can be solved, and then test that hypothesis by an actual experiment. Some flexible plan utilizing logical steps in problem solving is part of the preparation for any meeting. The actual steps can be described differently, but the most effective method is presented below.

Problem-Solving Guide

Problem-Solving Steps	Useful Member Roles	Blocks	Possible Methods
1. Defining the Problem	Orienting Clarifying Defining problem	Ambiguity Different perceptions Generalizations	Problem census Small groups Needs analysis
2. Checking Involvement	Testing Supporting Revealing interest	Silence "Yessing"	Going around the group Ranking priorities
3. Collecting Information and Diagnosis	Giving information Orienting Summarizing	Moving to next step Stepping too quickly Lack of focus	Force-field analysis Advance preparation Data collection
4. Suggesting Solutions	Seeking opinions Giving opinions Coordinating	Starting to evaluate ideas Limited participation Minority not heard	Brainstorming Small groups
5. Evaluating Alternatives	Giving opinions Testing feasibility Mediating-harmonizing Coordinating	Emotional distortions Conflicts Steamrolling Majority voting Loss of focus	Guided discussion Going around Force-field analysis Role playing Risk technique
6. Decision Making and Gaining Commitment	Giving opinions Coordinating Mediating-harmonizing Testing for consensus	Majority voting Polarizing Going along with group (no commitment)	Risk technique Provisional try Total-group discussion Protecting minority opinions
7. Planning Implementation	Giving information Testing feasibility Initiating	Lack of involvement Generalizations Vague responsibility	Implementation teams Small groups Committees
8. Evaluating/ Replanning	Coordinating Giving opinions Giving information	Expectations not clear Implementation Mechanics not clear	Work groups Committee reports Data collection

The greatest advantage of using logical steps in decision making is a separation of the suggesting of solutions from their discussion and, of course, this is where most groups get stuck. It is only natural that when a solution is suggested other members will reply with an opinion about the suggestion. This stopping and starting slows down the meeting, makes it difficult for all possible solutions to be stated, and tends to put the person suggesting the solution on the defensive. It does not allow for the various solutions to be compared with one another and rise or fall on their own merits. It is likely that the discussion leader will have to focus considerable attention on keeping these two steps separate in the group discussion. This can best be done by getting the group to agree to use such an approach before they get started and training them in the use of this approach during the meeting. The chairperson may point out deviations from the agreed-on procedures and encourage others to take responsibility to see that the problem-solving steps are followed in order.

The technique of brainstorming utilizes the logical steps in problem solving by clearly separating the suggestion of solutions from the discussion of their value. The basic rule in brainstorming is that no one can comment on or in any way belittle the suggestion of another member. The only response to another's suggestion that is allowed is building on it with another idea. This tends to increase the number and variety of suggested solutions, as the threat of having an idea "shot down" by the group is reduced. Much of the value of brainstorming can be achieved by separating step four (the suggesting of solutions) from step five (the discussion and testing of solutions) in the regular use of logical steps in problem solving.

Introducing the Discussion

A group meeting for the first time or with new members attending may need help in getting members acquainted. The chairperson should take on this responsibility or, at least, check to see that other members are carrying it out. This is the first step in establishing a warm, accepting climate that will facilitate the discussion. Other occasions may arise during the meeting for the chairperson to help members get to know each other personally. This is an important consideration, for we have seen that groups of friends or, at least, acquaintances have a higher degree of communication than groups of strangers.

Another function of the chairperson as the group comes together is to describe the structure for starting, stopping, breaking for coffee, and planning for future meetings. If previous arrangements in this area have not been made, the chairperson may help the group decide such matters at the opening or, perhaps, at a more opportune time during the discussion. The main point here is that the group becomes aware of the time available for them to work on the problem at hand.

In opening the meeting, the chairperson reviews the agenda for the session and, depending on the group's procedures, may ask for any new items or check the priority and order of the items presented. The chairperson or recorder may want to review material, decisions, or feelings left over from the last meeting. However, starting with "old business" is usually unwise, as it is rarely a priority item for participants and tends to sap energies with issues previously discussed. It is better to mobilize energy around the exciting topics for this meeting and create a positive, looking-ahead climate.

The area in which the group has freedom to make decisions is spelled out next. In many cases, this area of freedom will be how to carry out a certain requirement, rather than whether or not they want to do it. A club group, for example, is not asked what should be done about the mess they make during their meeting, but rather, how they want to make arrangements for cleaning up after their meeting. Members should know if they are free to make a decision, are being asked to give advice, or are just responding to a decision that has already been made. Very often the involvement of members can be increased at this stage of the discussion by having them participate in establishing or clarifying the goals and working out the plans for working toward these goals. The planner also helps the group to recognize other limitations, such as time, information, or equipment, within which they operate.

During the introduction stage, the chairperson takes great care to establish the emotional climate of trust, acceptance, and support that is so necessary to full communication, group freedom, and effective decision making. It is believed that this climate is best established by encouraging and accepting, reflecting and clarifying, and being nonjudgmental in repeating and summarizing statements. Establishing and maintaining this emotional climate limit the opportunity of the chairperson to express personal opinions during the discussion.

Defining the problem is usually much more difficult than it seems. A good way of checking on its clarity after it is presented is to ask a couple of members to describe their understanding of the problem. If people come back to problem clarification later in the meeting, it is another indication that it wasn't clearly understood at the beginning. Checking involvement or readiness to work on the problem is redundant if members have participated in setting up the agenda and prioritizing the items. But, as most groups don't do this, some kind of involvement checking is needed as the discussion starts.

Facilitating the Discussion

The major task of the chairperson and recorder in facilitating the discussion is to help the group to utilize logical steps in their decision-making procedures. In its early stages the group may train themselves in these procedures. The members will then have the skill to competently assume the responsibility for checking on their own procedures.

All members should help to encourage interaction in the group. A permissive, nonjudgmental climate and an informal atmosphere are helpful in encouraging members to discuss different points of view. The discussion leader watches for the feeling tone of contributions and does not become overly involved in the content. By watching unexpressed feelings, he is more able to get these out on the table at a later time for discussion by the group if they are getting in the way of the group reaching a decision. Experience suggests that it is more often the hidden agendas and unexpressed feelings that block the group coming to a decision than the actual differences in stated content. As the discussion leader encourages interaction, he has some responsibility to draw out the underparticipators and prevent the talkative members from dominating the discussion. The discussion leader may encourage underparticipators by saying, "Now we've had a few opinions; it would be helpful to hear from some of the others." Or, "What are some of the other ideas?" These general questions are more helpful than calling on individual members for an opinion or going around the group in order. Very often members do not have any particular opinion early in the discussion and to call for one from them may be forcing a judgment. It also puts them on record as favoring one approach or another and, if the judgment was forced, it may not reflect their true feelings. It is better to let them think through their own opinions as they hear others talk and come in with their thoughts when they feel ready to do so. Going around the group for opinions also tends to bring out the competitive aspect and make the discussion more a game to be won or lost than a meeting of minds to bring forth a solution that is better than any single proposal.

In a permissive atmosphere a variety of opinions on any subject are likely to come out. Discussion leaders can be helpful to the group by using their authority and example to recognize different opinions in as unbiased and nonjudgmental a fashion as possible. This encourages participation and also allows the group to sort through various suggestions (step five of our problem-solving sequence). It has also been demonstrated that a chairperson can raise the quality of a group's decision by encouraging the expression of minority opinion and protecting the minority opinion when it is under fire. The chairperson, in giving recognition to a minority opinion, enables it to be saved and used by the group if it is one of high quality. If, on the other hand, the suggestion is not a useful one, its recognition by the leader allows its originator to stop having to defend it. It is in the record and will rise and fall on its own merit. A member who does not have to defend an opinion because it has been recognized by the chairperson is more likely to consider other appropriate solutions.

As the group develops a free and permissive atmosphere, the members must be careful that they do not go too far and wander aimlessly in off-the-subject talk. As a group discussion gets off the track, a member, chairperson, or recorder may want to refocus the discussion with a question or two or, perhaps, ask the digressing members if they feel their points are related to the subject at hand. If they agree that the points are not directly related, their permission should be sought to bring them up after a conclusion on the point under discussion. Frequent evaluations by the group of the effectiveness of their procedures in reaching a group decision will help them learn from their own experience.

A group recorder is one of the most effective aids in helping a group keep its discussion on track and to know where it is in its sequence of problem-solving steps. The person in the group who acts as recorder keeps track of ideas and suggestions, of decisions reached, and the position of the group in respect to its agreed-on procedures or steps in problem solving. A group may frequently call on the recorder to restate the development of the discussion to that time or to summarize the major points made. For example, as a group moves from the stage of suggesting solutions to the stage of discussing those solutions, the recorder can remind the group of the proposals made and in this way helps to share the leadership load.

Groups often face decisions that involve new and different ways of doing things. A major problem in reaching agreement on decisions involving change is the fear members have about carrying out the decision and making the change. One approach, arising from the principle of reducing restraining forces, consists of having group members list the problems or risks that would be encountered in accepting the solution under discussion. For the time being, all of the positive aspects of the decision are set aside and the group concentrates on listing and analyzing its dangers and drawbacks. This may help the group, as it is usually more effective to reduce the drawbacks or forces working against a change rather than to try and strengthen or make more appealing the forces favoring that change.

Techniques to Help with Difficult Decisions

When difficult decisions are anticipated, there are a number of special techniques that build on increasing structure and focus as a way of increasing effectiveness and member satisfaction.

1. *Seating arrangements.* Control overparticipators by having them sit next to you. Encourage underparticipators by having them sit opposite you. Always sit where you have eye contact with each group member (if you don't, move or ask the person you can't see to move).

2. *Practicing for the meeting.* To prepare for the possible developments of a difficult meeting and be ready with contingency strategies, rehearse the meeting ahead of time. This could be done by fantasizing the meeting in your own mind and imagining all of the worst things that could happen and what you would do about them. Or, it could be done with the recorder or one or two other key members. A colleague not in the group could also be called on to be a consultant and play the "devil's advocate" and help you prepare for the meeting.

3. *Pro-con technique.* This is an extension of the force-field analysis described previously and asks the group to make up two lists: one of all the favorable factors and one of all the unfavorable factors concerning a specific issue or plan. The "risk technique" supplements this approach by focusing on all the reasons why this decision may not work and helps to surface the fears and risks that are restraining the decision.

4. *Rank-ordering decisions.* Once a number of decisions are proposed, or pro-con factors related to specific decisions are listed, it may help to rank order—list in order of importance—the items. The members do this individually and their rankings are combined to form an average group ranking. Or, the group may be given ten points and asked to distribute them among the items any way they choose. Thus, a member could assign all ten points to one proposal, or distribute the ten points among several proposed solutions.

5. *Process analysis.* If the meeting becomes blocked, stop it and ask the group to do a process analysis of what is happening. The recorder will be helpful here and you may want to assign an observer or two to help surface group dynamics.

6. *Going around the group.* If members become polarized and block progress, it is the uncommitted or neutral members who can be useful in breaking the deadlock. Going around the group and hearing from each member provides them an opportunity to be heard and perhaps propose solutions to break the deadlock.

7. *Private listing of opinions.* Opinions, ideas, or votes on a critical issue presented anonymously and in writing usually diffuse much of the emotion and confrontation of a verbal discussion. The "Delphi technique" and "nominal group technique" (Delbeq and others, 1975) build on this strategy.

8. *Subgrouping.* If the group is larger than twelve or fifteen people, it may help critical issues to be analyzed and summarized by dividing into groups of four to six to do it. Subgroups, because of their size, permit more air time per person and reduce the need to posture a position in front of the total group, as opinions are reported only on behalf of the small group.

9. *Breaks.* Schedule breaks or coffee time when emotions are counter-productive or the problem-solving sequence is blocked. Also be prepared to schedule a critical decision over two meetings: one to surface the issues, and one to make a group decision. The time between often helps to put the issues into fuller perspective and make a more rational decision.

10. *Check for hidden agendas.* In addition to the formal agenda with its clearly stated goals, there are often private and hidden personal agendas—motives, aspirations, biases—of individual members. For example, camp counselors may ask for an age group of campers based on their interest and ability with that age group, while hidden agendas are concerned with how early the campers go to bed (leaving the counselor free for the evening) or how willing they are to do the work around the cabin. Hidden agendas may also be related to status in the group, or antagonisms toward the leader or other group members. Surfacing hidden agendas usually reduces their blockages, although there are some that might hurt the group more if they were talked about.

Establishing Closure

If there is difficulty in reaching agreement on a decision, the discussion leader can encourage the different points of view to be re-explained and individuals can be encouraged to state their position. This is often helpful in getting the exact points of agreement and disagreement out into the open but has a drawback of lining up sides which appear to be in conflict. The chairperson or recorder can point out areas of agreement and disagreement, check for unexpressed opinions, and allow group pressure to work freely within the group. If it appears that personal feelings which have not been expressed are preventing agreements, the chairperson may want to get them into the discussion by asking members about the feelings that they have noticed, and possibly suggesting that they try to identify some of the hidden agendas which have been present during the meeting. Members can be asked to do "active listening" by requiring them to summarize the previous participator's points and check with this person that their summary is accurate before they can go on to make their own points.

If the group continues to be unable to reach agreement, the chairperson may want to state as a new problem the failure of the group to agree. "What will we do as a result of our failure to agree?" can be the new problem put to the group. As a last alternative, the discussion leader may suggest the problem be withdrawn, that the decision be postponed, that they try a provisional solution, accept a compromise, try alternating the proposed solutions on a trial basis, or actually sustain the majority solution, stating the drawbacks in this course of action.

Finally, the chairperson should give closure to the meeting either by summarizing the decisions (the recorder can also do this) or by helping the group evaluate its procedures. An announcement of time and plans for the next meeting, with any preparation that can be done for it, gives the members a sense of working ahead as they leave the meeting.

Process Evaluation Sessions

From time to time, and usually on some regular basis, the group should be encouraged to schedule process analysis periods. Some groups take ten minutes at the end of every meeting; other groups schedule process analysis for half a meeting once a month. At these times the group reviews how it is working and how members are feeling about the way it is working. Group evaluation forms or post-meeting questionnaires may be reviewed at this time. Some groups have a process observer who joins with the recorder in providing information for these sessions.

USING THE PROGRAM AS A TOOL FOR GROUP DEVELOPMENT

The activities of groups are often looked at as ends in themselves, and the kind of contribution they may make to the growth of the group is overlooked. However, each program in which a group participates influences, positively or negatively, how the members work with one another. Members may blow off steam with a strenuous activity, gain recognition through a community service project, create interpersonal friction through a group election, or become quite dependent on the worker while staging a rock festival. Though the effect of the activity varies with the group, common elements make prediction possible.

Sherif (1969), in his experiments with boys in a camp setting, has shown, for example, the effect of programs with a competitive element on group development. In one study, two fairly cohesive groups of boys were re-formed with each boy having more friends in the other group than in his own. After a few days of normal camp activities, most boys chose members of their new group as their best friends. Then the two groups came together in win-lose competitive games (such as a tug of war) and the result was negative attitudes between groups as former best friends now became aggressive enemies.

In a follow-up experiment, an attempt was made to reduce the intergroup conflict created by the win-lose competition by changing the activities and the interaction pattern between groups. Activities were introduced which required the cooperative efforts of all the boys in both groups for successful achievement. These activities reduced the intergroup friction and enabled the boys to begin to work together as a total group.

From my own camp experiences, two related situations stand out. Camps have difficulty getting campers for their last camp period, and large-scale, all-camp events are often put into the program during the last period to attract campers. One camp ran a week-long, all-camp competition where all members of the staff and campers were divided on a random basis into two teams and points were given for every conceivable camp activity and competition. The results of hostility and aggression, to say nothing of fatigue, were staggering. Under pressure from the staff, the camp finally abandoned this traditional competitive program. Another camp handled the same problem by putting on a large circus where every cabin group had a booth and entertained the rest of the camp. The result was increased cohesion of camp groups, as well as a greater identification with the camp as a whole. The program differed in a major dimension—a win-lose competition versus working together for the enjoyment of all.

Altering the program and the way in which members participate in the program is one of the major ways the worker can influence the group's vitality. By adding and subtracting activities, changing their balance and intensity, a significant change can often be effected in the major dimensions of a group's development.

Analysis of Development Potential in Activities

If activities are to be a tool used by the worker in enhancing the personal growth of group members, it is helpful to relate programs to the specific needs of the group. What programs are best for increasing cohesion? for encouraging responsibility? for getting out personal feelings within the group? Let us examine the range of dimensions that activities may contain.

1. *Interaction.* The degree to which an activity provides an opportunity for members to communicate and relate to one another.

2. *Limitations.* The extent to which programs have rules, specific ways of doing things, or limitations that will provide members an opportunity to test and explore them, or be free of them.

3. *Meeting individual needs.* What potential is there within the activity for members to find recognition, approval, a sense of belonging, and a feeling of accomplishment?

4. *Participation.* To what extent can the members plan, conduct, and follow up this activity?

5. *Worker role.* Is there any special role the worker will be expected to play or forced to play as part of this activity? (Selecting activities the members know allows the advisor to participate normally; selecting activities only he or she knows puts him or her in the role of teacher/instructor.)

6. *Expression of feelings.* What are the variations among activities regarding the extent to which they encourage members to express their feelings either directly (such as in discussions) or indirectly (such as through arts or dramatics)?

7. *Involvement.* The degree to which all members have an opportunity to be involved in the activity in an appropriate way. Can each member play a part in the activity that is within his or her repertoire of skills?

8. *Analysis of group and self.* To what extent does a program enable members to learn more about the group's operation, structure, and standards, as well as one's own role in the group and the effect on other members? Will an increased understanding of the group and self be a product of this activity?

9. *Structure.* The degree to which there is an established way of carrying out an activity. Painting a picture by numbers or completing a jigsaw puzzle are examples of highly structured activities. Finger painting and clay modeling are rather unstructured activities. Members should have an opportunity to test themselves and learn to function effectively in both situations.

10. *Authority.* How much does an activity enable members to explore their relationship with an authority figure in order to work through feelings of dependence and independence, and learn interdependence?

Activities for Building Group Cohesion

Factors likely to increase group cohesion include attraction to the group based on personal friendships, interesting activities, and group status. Activities with high interaction potential are most likely to help strengthen friendships within a group. High-interaction activities include most games, projects, discussions, planning sessions, and sports. Low-interaction activities include sports such as swimming and games where members are eliminated from play because they are "caught." Some arts and crafts projects are of an individual nature and tend to limit interaction. Spectator activities (watching a film or listening to a speaker) also have low interaction potential.

Activities Increasing Understanding of Self and Others

The best activities here are those that provide for the exposure of the attitudes and behavior of each of the members and are followed up by one of several methods of analysis that will increase sensitivity and understanding. Activities that allow a great deal of individual behavior to be expressed include most programs where the members are responsible for planning and carrying out action steps. Such activities can become vehicles for increasing understanding of self and others by adding an analysis or follow-up session where members have a chance to discuss the behavior of themselves and others. This may often be done through an evaluation of the program itself, analyzing its weaknesses and strengths, and looking at some of the things that individuals did which were most helpful. The member and group rating instruments described in Parts 2 and 3 can be used at this time to increase understanding. For example, the Survey of Group Development is a useful tool to open up a discussion of the group's structure. Later, as the group becomes more comfortable in discussing itself, focus can begin to shift to the roles and behavior of the individual members.

Activities Encouraging Expression and Creativity

Unstructured activities, such as singing, skits, dancing, and open discussions, are natural methods of group expression. Creativity-oriented activities are also low in structure and must provide opportunities for individual differences. Activities that have expected finished products are less useful than open-ended ones for encouraging creativity. Member-created skits provide more creative opportunities than learning the formal lines of an established play. Finger painting and clay modeling are more flexible than painting by numbers or putting together a model from a commercial kit.

Activities Enabling Members to Experiment with Authority, Structure, and Limitations

Activities with a high potential in these areas are ones that have specific rules, involve interaction with the worker, and are either very high or very low in structure. Sports and games provide opportunities to deal with rules. High on the list are games with rules that require a judgment either by the players or by a referee. Basketball, volleyball, baseball, and relay races are examples of these games. Other activities may give occasion for experiencing limitations where there are tools or materials to share, turns to be taken, or limited time available for the activity. Games or situations where members are likely to be penalized (such as a foul in basketball or hockey) provide for the testing of limits. Agency rules and regulations are subject to testing by members.

Activities for experimenting with authority require the worker to interact with the members. Various worker roles of being referee, coach, arbitrator, teacher or instructor, organizer, and regular participant provide the most scope for relating to authority figures. Games may put the worker into a referee position; sports require a coach; dramatics and arts and crafts, a critic; and agency-group problems press the worker into an arbitration role. These are, however, the roles that authority people most commonly play at home, school, and work. The unique experience that group service agencies can provide is to work with an authority figure who is a helper and a teacher or organizer. To be able to work out rules, solve disagreements, and learn new activities without the worker running the show is the new element of the experience for most members. In fact, having an opportunity to work out a group program from scratch with a worker who does not dominate the process or tell members what to do has proven to be one of the most useful programs for working through relations with authority figures and learning the flexibility that unstructured situations require.

This sample of learning goals and activities serves to illustrate the possibilities of starting from group goals and selecting activities that are most likely to satisfy them. In this way, the program becomes an important technique in facilitating group growth.

BIBLIOGRAPHY

Bennis, W. G., K. Benne & R. Chin (eds.). *The Planning of Change.* New York: Holt, Rinehart & Winston, 1976.

Bradford, Leland P. (ed.). *Group Development.* San Diego, CA: University Associates, 1978.

Delbeq, A., A. Van de Ven & D. Gustafson. *Group Techniques for Program Planning.* Glenview, IL: Scott, Foresman, 1975.

Dimock, Hedley G. *Intervention and Collaborative Change.* Guelph, Ontario: University of Guelph, 1981.

Dimock, Hedley G. The use of System Improvement Research in developing a change strategy in human service organizations. In *Group and Organization Studies,* 3: 365-375, 1978.

Gulley, Halbert E. *Discussion, Conference and Group Process.* New York: Holt, Rinehart & Winston, 1960, 1968, 1977.

Hornstein, H. and others (eds.). *Social Intervention.* New York: Free Press, 1971.

Janis, I. and L. Mann. *Decision Making.* New York: Free Press, 1977.

Maier, Norman R.F. *Problem Solving Discussions and Conferences.* New York: McGraw-Hill, 1963.

Sherif, Muzafer & Carolyn Sherif. *Social Psychology.* New York: Harper & Row, 1969.

Sorenson, Roy & Hedley S. Dimock. *Designing Education in Values.* New York: Association Press, 1955.

Zander, Alvin. *Making Groups Effective.* San Francisco: Jossey-Bass, 1982.